DISEASES
3rd Revised Edition

Volume 6

Mumps to Polycythemia

Bryan Bunch
and
Jenny Tesar
EDITORS

GROLIER
an imprint of
◾SCHOLASTIC
Scholastic Library Publishing
www.scholastic.com/librarypublishing

Editors: Bryan Bunch and Jenny Tesar, Scientific Publishing

Design and production: G & H SOHO, Inc.
  Design: Gerry Burstein
  Prepress: Kathie Kounouklos

Writers:

Barbara Branca
Bryan Bunch
Barbara A. Darga
Betsy Feist
Gene R. Hawes
Wendy B. Murphy
Karin L. Rhines
Jenny Tesar
Bruce Wetterau
Gray Williams

Editorial assistant:
Marianne Bunch

Copyediting:
Felice Levy

Index
Felice Levy and Marianne Bunch

Creative assistance:
Pam Forde

Illustrators:

Photography supervisor:
Karin L. Rhines

Photographs:
Karin L. Rhines *(except where noted)*

Icons:
Steve Virkus and Karen Presser

Medical Illustrations:
Jean Cassels, Leslie Dunlap, Pamela Johnson, and Joel Snyder

Library of Congress Cataloging-in-Publication Data

Diseases / Bryan Bunch and Jenny Tesar, editors. — 3rd rev. ed.
    p. cm.
    Includes index.
    Summary: Alphabetically arranged articles presenting medical
    information on more than 500 diseases, discussing causes, symptoms,
    stages of the disease, its likelihood of striking, treatments, prevention,
    and long-term effects.
    ISBN 0-7172-6205-7 (set) — ISBN 0-7172-6206-5 (v. 1) — ISBN
0-7172-6207-3 (v. 2) — ISBN 0-7172-6208-1 (v. 3) — ISBN 0-7172-6209-X
(v. 4) — ISBN 0-7172-6210-3 (v. 5) — ISBN 0-7172-6211-1 (v. 6) — ISBN
0-7172-6212-X (v. 7) — ISBN 0-7172-6213-8 (v. 8)   1. Diseases —
Encyclopedias, Juvenile.   I. Bunch, Bryan H.   II. Tesar, Jenny E.

R130.5.D57   2006
616.003—dc22   2006007986

Third revised edition published 2006, by Scholastic Library Publishing.
First published in the United States in 1997 by
Grolier Educational, Sherman Turnpike, Danbury, CT 06816

COPYRIGHT © 2006, 2003, 1997 by SCIENTIFIC PUBLISHING, INC.

Set ISBN-10: 0-7172-6205-7
Set ISBN-13: 978-0-7172-6205-2

Volume ISBN-10: 0-7172-6211-1
Volume ISBN-13: 978-0-7172-6211-3

Mumps

DISEASE

TYPE: INFECTIOUS (VIRAL)

On the Internet
KIDS HEALTH
kidshealth.org/parent/infections/
bacterial_viral/mumps.html

Though mumps, sometimes called "the mumps," can make a child very uncomfortable, it is not usually a serious disease in children. Adult cases have more severe symptoms and occasional complications.

Cause: Mumps is caused by a spherically shaped virus of the genus *Paramyxovirus.* The virus lives only in humans and is transmitted from one person to another by droplets of saliva expelled during a cough or sneeze. Direct contact with infected saliva also spreads the infection.

Incidence: Mumps is most likely to affect unvaccinated children between the ages of six and fourteen. In parts of the world where vaccination has not been required, including Poland and China, childhood mumps is still epidemic, with tens of thousands of cases each year. People who have had the disease, however, are almost always immune for life.

Introduction of the first live-virus vaccine in 1967 and subsequent improvements in vaccines have reduced incidence of mumps in nations with mandatory vaccination to about 1% of incidence in the 1960s. However, in 2006 an epidemic of mumps struck the U.S. Midwest, infecting especially teenagers and college students. In many cases, those infected had only one of the recommended two vaccinations.

Noticeable symptoms: Swelling of the largest salivary glands, known as the *parotid* (puh-ROT-ihd) *glands,* is the most common symptom of mumps. This swelling may make cheeks puff out and cause discomfort, especially while eating. The other salivary glands also swell but are not so prominent.

The mumps virus sometimes infects parts of the body besides the salivary glands, such as the pancreas. Males past the age of puberty infected with the mumps may experience infected testicles. Females may suffer swelling of their ovaries, though this symptom is rare. The ears and hearing can be affected. The most serious complication of mumps occurs in the rare cases when the virus causes inflammation of the brain, which can be life-threatening.

Sometimes foods and drinks that are acidic irritate the swollen glands. There may also be a fever of anywhere from

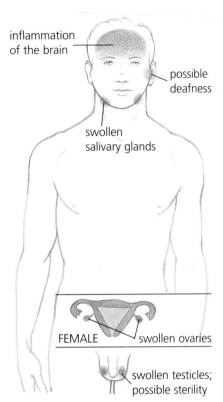

inflammation
of the brain

possible
deafness

swollen
salivary glands

FEMALE   swollen ovaries

swollen testicles;
possible sterility

Mumps nearly always causes swelling and pain in the salivary glands. It may affect the organs directly involved in reproduction, cause inflammation of the brain, or produce permanent hearing loss.

100° to 104°F, headache, and back pain. Often there is diarrhea and the general flulike symptoms caused by the struggle between the immune system and a virus. However, a person can have the mumps without showing any symptoms at all; this happens in about a third of the cases.

Diagnosis: Often a doctor will be able to diagnose mumps on the basis of the patient's age, swollen salivary glands, and the physician's knowledge that a number of children at the patient's school have come down with the disease. If confirmation of the diagnosis is needed, a blood or saliva sample can be tested for presence of the mumps virus.

Treatment options: As is the case with most diseases caused by a virus, physicians do not have any specific treatment for mumps other than bed rest if the patient has a temperature and an analgesic, such as acetaminophen, for pain.

All patients should be isolated to prevent infecting anyone who has not had the disease. Mumps is usually contagious from about one day before the swelling begins to five or more days after.

Stages and progress: Generally, it takes two to three weeks after infection for the first signs of salivary gland swelling to appear. Swelling of the salivary gland or glands may last for seven to ten days, and the patient can run a fever for anywhere from one to six days. If pancreatitis occurs, it will cause a stomachache that lasts for two or three days.

For about one in five males with mumps, especially those over ten years of age, one or both testicles may become inflamed and swollen—usually just one. This can be painful, reduce fertility, and, on rare occasions, cause sterility. Swollen testicles from mumps may increase the risk of testicular cancer. About one in twenty females with mumps may have inflamed ovaries. The disease sometimes affects the glands in women's breasts.

Another potentially serious complication is inflammation of the brain—encephalitis or meningitis—in roughly 10% of cases. Dizziness, vomiting, headache, and lethargy are symptoms of this condition. Usually, brain inflammation clears up by itself with no permanent damage, but on rare occasions it can be fatal. Other glands or organs are rarely infected.

Although permanent deafness from mumps is now rare—about one in 15,000 cases, usually in one ear—mumps was a leading cause of deafness in the past.

Prevention: Mumps vaccine provides long-lasting immunity in about 90% of all people who receive it.

People who have not been vaccinated and have never had the mumps should stay away from anyone infected with the disease until the swelling subsides and the danger of infection has passed.

Get vaccinated

Muscles

Much of what we call flesh or meat consists of organs known as muscles. When almost any part of the body moves, whether as a result of a conscious decision or during a life process such as respiration or digestion, the motion occurs because of a change in the length of a muscle. Individual cells, such as macrophages, however, move by different processes that do not use muscles.

Size and location: There are between 400 and 650 muscles in the body that have been named (lists vary considerably). They occur in three different systems.

■ *Skeletal muscles:* These are what one normally thinks of as muscles. Skeletal muscles are attached to bones of the skeleton. They are made from fibers that are striped—or *striated* (STRIY-AY-tihd)—in appearance under a microscope; thus they are also called *striated muscles.* Each fiber can contract or lengthen when the muscle receives a message from the brain. Because the mind controls the use of these muscles, they are also known as *voluntary muscles.* The skeletal muscles usually occur in pairs, one contracting while the other relaxes.

■ *Smooth muscles:* These are found in the walls of the stomach and intestines, in the walls of veins and arteries, and in various other internal organs. They are for the most part not directed by the will, so they are also known as the *involuntary muscles.* People do have partial control over some of the involuntary muscles, however; for example, you can stop the smooth muscle of the diaphragm from causing you to breathe for a time.

■ *Cardiac muscles:* The muscles found in the heart appear similar to striated muscles, but are connected differently. In oper-

Muscle tissue responds to regular use against a force by increasing the size of individual cells in the muscle, making the cells stronger and able to withstand repeated action for longer periods of time.

skeletal (voluntary, striped)

smooth (involuntary)

cardiac (involuntary, striped)

contracted triceps   relaxed biceps   contracted biceps

relaxed triceps

ation they move independently and will continue to contract for a time even if heart tissue is kept alive outside the body when no nerve message reaches the muscle tissue at all.

By weight muscles are about 40% of a man's body, but only about 30% of most women's bodies. These ratios can be changed by exercise, however, since muscles grow in size and weight with use (see Hypertrophy).

Role: The muscles function using a system of contractions of the different fibers that form each muscle. In normal use some of the fibers in any muscle are partly contracted. This state of partial contraction is called *muscle tone.* For movement to occur a muscle must elongate (relax) or shorten (contract). This is an all-or-nothing situation; there are no degrees of contraction. Continuous motion is accomplished by a complex pattern of some fibers shortening while others wait their turn. Each contract-relax cycle is a brief *twitch.* Although each fiber only contracts for a short time and then relaxes, the whole muscle can be shortened for quite a long period of time. But if, for example, muscles lift a large weight, the fibers soon begin to rebel against twitching over and over. The muscles tire, and the person receives a message from the muscles to put the weight down.

Muscles are one of the main differences between nearly all animals and other creatures in the world, such as plants, funguses, and bacteria. A plant can move slowly by growing more cells in one place than in another; or somewhat faster by changing the pressure of a fluid. But most animals can move parts of their bodies with great speed. One result is that animals live by consuming plants and other animals.

The difference is deeper than that, however. Complex animals have many internal organs that can process the food that their speed enables them to capture and that can move nutrients quickly around their bodies to nourish fast-acting muscle

The three types of muscle look different when their fibers are viewed under a microscope. But all the muscles work when the fibers shorten, causing the muscles to contract, or return to their original state, causing the muscles to relax. Skeletal muscles often come in pairs, so that one contracts as its partner relaxes.

cells, among other body cells. Thus the three types of muscle work together to make the animal lifestyle possible.

Conditions that affect the muscles: Muscle contractions are partly controlled by calcium, used to carry electrical charges into and out of cells. Calcium is nearly always available as the body takes calcium from bone if the supply gets low. If the supply fails, however, the muscle fibers contract all at once. Sometimes other conditions can cause such a contraction, which is fatal if it continues for any length of time. The best known is tetanus, also called *lockjaw* because the jaw muscles tighten and close the mouth. Some poisons produce the same condition, notably strychnine (STRIHK-niyn).

Muscle pain sometimes develops for no known cause, although emotional stress may be a factor. This sort of pain, more common in older people, is sometimes termed *fibrositis* (FIY-bruh-SIY-tihs).

A group of common genetic diseases that attack muscles are those categorized as muscular dystrophy. Several diseases that attack the nerves also cause muscles to fail and eventually atrophy. Among these are ALS, multiple sclerosis, and myasthenia gravis. The origin of these diseases is somewhat mysterious, although all seem to be at least partly caused by reactions of the immune system against the nerves.

Muscular dystrophy
(DIHS-truh-fee)

DISEASE

TYPE: GENETIC

Muscular dystrophy is a group of several genetic diseases with the same basic symptom: the progressive wasting of muscles. Two of these diseases, *Duchenne* (doo-SHEHN) *muscular dystrophy* and *Becker muscular dystrophy,* are most common, while three other forms also occur. Duchenne and Becker muscular dystrophy affect males almost exclusively and result from mutations within the same gene.

Duchenne muscular dystrophy is at once the most common and most serious form. It is a relentless and catastrophic disease that first becomes evident in childhood, as early as age three. It first attacks the muscles of the hips and legs: The affected child loses the ability to run or jump and has increasing difficulty in walking or climbing stairs. By ages seven to twelve the child is likely to lose the ability to walk altogether

On the Internet
NATIONAL INSTITUTE
OF NEUROLOGICAL DISORDERS
AND STROKE
www.ninds.nih.gov/disorders/
md/md.htm

and suffers the weakening of many other muscle groups. He becomes progressively helpless, with a weakened heart, breathing difficulties, and susceptibility to respiratory infections.

About a third of those affected have learning disabilities or show signs of mild to moderate developmental disability (mental retardation). Unlike the wasting of the muscles, however, the mental conditions do not get worse over time.

Becker muscular dystrophy is a milder disorder in just about every respect. It appears later—during adolescence or even adulthood. An affected boy may remain able to walk until he is an adult and may never have to use a wheelchair at all.

Cause: Both Duchenne and Becker muscular dystrophy are caused by defects in a single protein molecule called *dystrophin*. The protein is found mainly in muscle cells, although a slightly different form occurs in the brain. A boy with Duchenne muscular dystrophy has little or no dystrophin in his body. A boy with the Becker form has less of the protein than normal, or the molecule is abnormal in some way.

Just how the protein defects result in muscle breakdown is not yet understood. The deformation and destruction of the cells apparently start at birth, but at first the tissue regenerates fast enough to make up for the damage. That is why obvious symptoms do not appear for some years.

The gene for dystrophin is on the X chromosome, and the patterns of inheritance for both Duchenne and Becker muscular dystrophy are X-linked (see Genetic diseases). Thus, with only a few exceptions, only boys have the disease.

Incidence: Duchenne muscular dystrophy occurs in about 1 in 3,500 to 4,000 boys. Becker muscular dystrophy is considerably less common, occurring in about 1 in 30,000 boys.

Noticeable symptoms: Symptoms of Duchenne muscular dystrophy appear early but gradually. The muscles at the hips are likely to be the first affected. The toddler may seem unusually clumsy. His walk may be odd from the start, with feet kept wide apart to maintain a precarious balance. He may fall easily and have trouble getting up. He is also likely to have progressive difficulty in running, jumping, and climbing stairs. To maintain his balance, he will tend to thrust his abdomen forward and draw his shoulders back.

Other characteristic symptoms accompany the progressive destruction of the muscles. Early on, for example, the calves of the legs are likely to swell, as if the muscles were growing unusually fast. In fact, this *pseudohypertrophy* ("false over-growth") is made up of fat and connective tissue, not muscle, and has no strength.

The progression of symptoms in Becker muscular dystrophy is somewhat similar, but the symptoms appear much later and tend to be less pronounced. While the same pseudo-hypertrophy of the calves is likely to appear, heart damage and developmental disability are less common.

Diagnosis: One of the earliest effects of both Duchenne and Becker muscular dystrophy is a weakening of muscle cell membranes; this allows enzymes normally contained in the cells to leak into the blood. One of these enzymes, *creatine kinase,* is easily detected in a blood sample. Boys with Duchenne muscular dystrophy show enormously high levels of the enzyme, particularly in their first years; those with Becker muscular dystrophy are likely to have noticeably high levels. Testing for creatine kinase is one of the methods used to diagnose muscular dystrophy in babies suspected from family history to be at risk.

The gene for dystrophin is very large, and it can be made abnormal by many different mutations in the long chain of its DNA. So DNA analysis is mainly practical in families with several affected members whose DNA can be analyzed to find the specific mutation causing the disease. Furthermore, at least a third of all cases of muscular dystrophy are believed to result from some new mutation of the gene within the mother's egg.

Treatment options: Muscular dystrophy cannot be cured at this time. Physical therapy, corticosteroid drugs, mechanical aids such as braces and wheelchairs, and even surgery are used to prolong mobility as long as possible.

Outlook: A boy with Duchenne muscular dystrophy usually dies in his early twenties from failure of essential muscles, or from a respiratory infection such as pneumonia. For those with Becker muscular dystrophy, life span is likely to be somewhat shortened, but most affected men survive into their forties or fifties.

Myasthenia gravis

(MIY-uhs-THEE-nee-uh GRAAV-ihs)

DISEASE

TYPE: AUTOIMMUNE

See also
Autoimmune diseases
Immune system
Lymphocytes
Thymus

On the Internet
MAYO CLINIC
www.mayoclinic.com/health/
myasthenia-gravis/DS00375

Did You Know?
Although the thymus is often called the thymus gland, it does not produce a hormone. Instead, it is an important part of the immune system.

Drooping eyelids, fuzzy vision, and weakening muscles may be symptoms of myasthenia gravis ("serious muscle disease"). In this disease transmission of nerve impulses to muscles is impaired. As a result the muscles contract less efficiently.

Cause: The normal function of antibodies is to attack foreign invaders. Instead, in myasthenia gravis certain antibodies attack the parts of the protein in muscles that are responsible for picking up messages from nerves. This interferes with transmission of the messages and prevents the muscles from responding fully.

Scientists do not yet understand how this process starts. A majority of patients have an enlarged thymus, and 10 to 15% have benign tumors of the thymus, called thymomas (thiy-MOH-muhs). The thymus has an important role in the immune system, helping train white blood cells, which produce antibodies, about the distinction between self and nonself.

Incidence: Estimates of the prevalence of myasthenia gravis vary widely, ranging from about 15,000 to 60,000 people in the United States. Women most often develop the disease in their late teens and twenties; for men, the onset usually occurs after age 60.

A significant percentage of babies born to mothers with myasthenia gravis have muscle weakness called *neonatal* (NEE-oh-NAYT-l) *myasthenia;* in most cases the symptoms disappear within a few weeks.

Noticeable symptoms: Muscles that control the face and mouth are most severely affected. Drooping of upper eyelids and double vision usually are the first signs. Difficulty in swallowing and in pronouncing words may also occur. As the disease progresses, weakening of muscles may make breathing, walking, and other activities difficult.

No stress

Diagnosis: Rest lessens the muscle fatigue of myasthenia gravis. Therefore, if a physician suspects this disease, tests will be conducted to determine the effects of exercise and subsequent rest on muscle fatigue. Blood tests and electromyography, in which the nerves are stimulated, may be used to confirm the diagnosis. A CT or MRI scan may be used to examine the thymus.

Treatment options: There is no known cure but medications can help relieve symptoms. Muscle function can often be restored with cholinesterase inhibitors, which increase nerve signal transmission. Immune-system suppressors fight the harmful antibodies. During severe attacks, the patient's blood plasma may be replaced with plasma that does not contain such antibodies. Thymectomy (thiy-MEHK-tuh-mee)—removal of the thymus—is a common option that succeeds best with younger patients.

Stress of all types should be avoided when possible. Resting when muscle weakness sets in can help restore strength.

Mycoplasmal pneumonia *See* **Pneumonia**

Myocardial infarction *See* **Heart attack**

Myocarditis
(MIY-oh-kahr-DIY-tihs)

DISEASE

TYPE: INFECTIOUS; CHEMICAL; AUTOIMMUNE

On the Internet
MEDLINE PLUS
www.nlm.nih.gov/medlineplus/
ency/article/000149.htm

Myocarditis is an inflammation of the *myocardium,* or heart muscle.

Cause: The initial symptoms of myocarditis are directly caused by a bacterial, viral, parasitic, or fungus infection. The "strep" infection rheumatic fever is one cause of heart defects, but anything that produces inflammation of the heart muscle, including chemical poisoning, results in myocarditis. It can be a complication of several medications.

If myocarditis continues beyond the initial attack, it is probably the result of an attack by the immune system on heart muscle. A virus may have caused heart muscle cell proteins to enter the blood. The body's immune system attacks the protein in the blood and also in the heart, causing the heart tissue to

See also
Autoimmune diseases
Heart
Heart failure
Inflammation
"Strep"
Viruses and disease

become inflamed and damaged. The heart's electrical system and its ability to pump blood may then be impaired.

Incidence: Myocarditis is uncommon, striking fewer than 10 out of every 100,000 persons. It occurs in people of all ages, but about half the patients are younger than 40.

Noticeable symptoms: Mild cases may produce no symptoms other than those of the underlying disorder. Symptoms that do occur vary widely. They may include fatigue, shortness of breath, rapid or irregular heartbeat, or fever. In severe cases there may be strong chest pain or lung congestion.

Diagnosis: The combination of an infectious illness with rapid or irregular heartbeats or chest pain suggests the possibility of myocarditis. A chest x-ray and an ECG, or electrocardiogram, will show whether the heart is enlarged or damaged and reveal any problems in the heart's electrical activity. An echocardiogram produces images of the heart's four chambers and indicates the strength of the contractions. In very severe cases a heart biopsy may be needed. A very small piece of heart muscle tissue is surgically removed and then examined under a microscope.

Treatment options: Antibiotics are often sufficient to eliminate the underlying cause in the case of a bacterial infection. Other drugs may be prescribed to control inflammation or prevent clots. Immune suppression has helped prevent chronic myocarditis. If the heart has been severely damaged, valve replacements or a heart transplant may be required.

Stages and progress: There is often spontaneous recovery, but if untreated, myocarditis may permanently damage heart muscle tissue and heart valves or lead to congestive heart failure.

Prevention: Keep immunizations current. Influenza, polio, and other viral diseases are frequent instigators, as is diphtheria.

Get vaccinated

Myopia　　　*See* **Eyes and vision**

Myxedema　　　*See* **Hormone disorders**

N

Nail infections and injuries

Emergency Room

Infection of the skin around the fingernail or toenail, known as *paronychia* (PAAR-uh-NIHK-ee-uh), or fungal infection of the nail itself, can lead to deformity of the affected nail. Physical injury to a nail, from poorly fitted shoes or from hiking down a mountain, for example, can cause bleeding under the nail. This condition is called *subungual* (suhb-UNG-gwuhl) *hematoma*. Partial separation of a nail from the finger or toe is known as *onycholysis* (ON-ih-KOL-ih-sihs). This condition may result in considerable discomfort, make the nail appear black or yellow, and open the way for infection. The injured nail may even die and then be pushed off by the new nail that grows in. An ingrown toenail, often the result of improper trimming of a nail, may also cause a painful infection of the toe.

Cause: When the skin around the nails becomes infected, it is usually caused by staphylococcus bacteria or by a fungus. The infection often strikes people who frequently immerse their hands in water and detergent. Splitting, brittleness, or peeling can also be caused by strong soaps or certain chemicals, including nail polish remover.

A number of illnesses can deform nails. Among these are skin diseases such as psoriasis and eczema. Often diseases that seem to have little to do with the nails, such as heart disease or cancer, have nail injury or deformation as a side effect.

Noticeable symptoms: Bacterial infections around the nail usually appear suddenly and can be quite painful. The skin turns red and swells up; pus may ooze from the area. Often a nail that is injured will turn black from blood oozing below it or from bacteria growing beneath it. It may turn yellow when there is onycholysis. White patches usually result from a minor injury; they gradually move to the end of a nail and disappear.

Fingernails can be protected against various types of infection simply by wearing water-resistant gloves when the hands will be wet, as when washing dishes.

Treatment options: Both bacterial and fungal paronychia are usually treated with oral medications such as antibiotics or itraconazole, although yeast infections (*Candida*) are treated with topical creams. If a nail problem results from some other disease, the underlying disease will be treated if possible. Injuries to nails are usually self-correcting, given time, but it may be necessary to relieve pressure by piercing the nail if there is bleeding under it.

Bacterial infections can spread all the way around the nail and then work their way under the nail as well. In advanced cases the nail may fall off, and bacteria may even enter the bloodstream. ***Get medical attention promptly if you notice red lines leading away from an infected nail.*** This is a sign that bacteria have entered the bloodstream.

Prevention: Keep nails clean and dry. Wearing rubber gloves whenever you will be getting your hands wet can help prevent infections of the skin around nails. Be sure to dust the inside of the gloves with talc or wear cotton gloves inside the rubber gloves to prevent an allergic reaction. Moisturize, then gently push back the skin at the base of the nails (the cuticle). Never cut the cuticle because this can open the way to bacterial infection.

Nailing down a diagnosis

Often a physician will take a person's hand during a general physical examination and look first at one side and then the other. The doctor is looking for various signs, including the temperature and moistness of the skin. But one important clue to ill health that an observant physician seeks is the condition of the fingernails.

Nails may thicken as the result of poor circulation caused by hardening of the arteries. Spoon-shaped nails are a sign of iron-deficiency anemia. Anemia can also cause the nails to be pale with ridges running parallel to the finger or toe, while chronic liver disease can produce white nails against the yellow background of jaundice. White bands across nails indicate a protein deficiency. Congenital heart disease, as well as lung infections and lung cancer, cause the ends of the fingers and toes to become enlarged and knobby and the nails to widen or turn down at the ends, or both. Certain lung and heart diseases turn the nail bed bluish gray, and infections of the heart valves as well as some autoimmune diseases, including lupus, cause small black patches to appear under the nails. A groove across the nails may appear after an illness of any kind. It will eventually disappear.

Nanomedicine

REFERENCE

See also
Diagnostic tests
Genetic engineering
Medications
Prostheses ("replacement body parts")

On the Internet
NATIONAL INSTITUTES
OF HEALTH
Roadmap for Medical Research
http://nihroadmap.nih.gov/
nanomedicine/

Did You Know?

Richard Feynman, a Nobel-Prize-winning physicist, suggested in 1959 that useful tools could be made at very small scales, even from just a few atoms. This is considered the birth of nanotechnology.

In the 1966 fictional movie *Fantastic Voyage*, physicians were shrunk to the size of human cells so that they could journey through a human body and remove a blood clot causing a stroke. Today, real scientists are shrinking devices and structures even smaller than that to cure disease or to repair damaged tissues at the level of molecules. This emerging technology is called nanomedicine.

Nanomedicine's name is based on the combining form *nano-*, which means "a billionth." A nanometer is a billionth of a meter, and the tools and structures of nanomedicine are less than a hundred nanometers in length. For comparison, one atom is about a tenth of a nanometer in diameter, while a large virus may be 100 nanometers across.

Tools: Miniature imaging devices of various kinds have been developed. One example is a pill that, when swallowed, takes pictures every few seconds while it passes through the digestive system.

Many of the new tools of nanomedicine are sensors, often nanoparticles engineered to glow when a particular situation is encountered, such as low blood sugar, cancer cells, or radiation. Nanosensors on the faces of surgical tools allow a surgeon to work with greater precision and safety.

Other devices stimulate individual nerves with electric signals, including nerves involved in seeing or hearing to restore sight or sound detection. Tools that physically manipulate individual molecules are still in the planning stages. One example is an artificial red blood cell that would transport gases more efficiently than natural red blood cells.

Materials: Substances in tiny amounts behave differently from their properties in bulk. Nanomedicine materials are powders made from tiny structures with engineered characteristics. For example, some nanoscale medicines enter cells without triggering an immune response. Pastes made from nanoparticles used for bone repair can be stronger than ordinary materials.

Silver has been known since ancient times to possess antibiotic properties, but close contact between particles of silver and bacteria is required. Catheters or other surgical devices that are inserted into the body often develop thin layers of bacteria that then cause infection or disease. Coating devices with silver nanoparticles prevents bacteria from attaching.

Narcolepsy

(NAHR-kuh-LEHP-see)

People who have narcolepsy suffer uncontrollable episodes in which they suddenly fall asleep for anywhere from a few minutes to several hours.

Cause: Doctors do not know exactly what causes narcolepsy.

Incidence: An estimated 200,000 Americans suffer narcolepsy. Symptoms of the disorder usually first appear when a person is between 15 and 25 years of age, often because he or she is having trouble staying awake in classes at school.

Noticeable symptoms: Although narcolepsy can be recognized by characteristic abrupt shifts from waking directly into deep sleep, many people with this disease think they are normal, but just fall asleep easily. Only about one in four persons with narcolepsy also suffers more dramatic symptoms: These include sudden attacks of muscle weakness, waking or sleeping. Called *cataplexy* (KAAT-uh-PLEHK-see), this condition may even cause the victim to fall and remain unable to move for some time. While falling asleep or waking up, the person with narcolepsy encounters brief periods of paralysis, called *sleep paralysis*. Dreams are often unusually vivid.

Diagnosis: The first order is to show that other disorders, such as restless leg syndrome or sleep apnea, are not the cause. An electroencephalogram may be used to observe brain waves during sleep. Abnormal versions of a stage of sleep called *rapid-eye-movement* (REM) *sleep* is a major symptom. Other physiological functions during sleep may also be monitored.

Treatment: Doctors usually recommend behavioral changes and prescribe central nervous system stimulants to help combat sleep attacks and antidepressants to improve the quality of REM sleep.

Prevention: Getting adequate sleep at night is an important part of preventing unexpected sleep episodes. Scheduling brief naps during the day, avoiding heavy meals, and drinking coffee, tea, and other beverages containing caffeine can also help.

> **Did You Know?**
> Research in narcolepsy is conducted mainly with dogs that have the disease. When presented with a treat or other excitement, the dogs fall into a narcoleptic sleep similar to that of humans with the disease.

Nausea

(NAW-zee-uh)

SYMPTOM

Emergency Room

Call ambulance

Nausea refers to the very unpleasant, queasy feeling that you are going to throw up the contents of your stomach, or *vomit*.

Related symptoms: Vomiting can follow nausea; or the "dry heaves," retching without bringing up stomach contents, may occur. Nausea often accompanies headache—sometimes nausea causes headache, while some kinds of headache produce nausea. Heartburn or indigestion may also mix with nausea.

Associations: Nausea originates from many different situations, conditions, and diseases, including the following, arranged to some degree in order of the seriousness of the underlying condition:

- emotional stress, including the stress of speaking or performing in public
- unpleasant odors, especially rotting flesh
- overeating or eating rich foods containing butter or cream
- pregnancy ("morning sickness")
- motion sickness or seasickness
- drinking too much alcohol
- chemotherapy or radiation therapy
- viral diseases such as "stomach flu" (viral gastroenteritis), mumps, or a persistent cold
- heat exhaustion
- mountain sickness or altitude sickness (polycythemia)
- migraine headache
- illnesses that inflame the esophagus or stomach lining *(If you see blood in vomit, unusual colors, such as green or yellow, or a substance resembling coffee grounds, call your doctor or go to an emergency room at once.)*
- food poisoning
- acute glaucoma *(When accompanied by severe pain around one eye and blurred vision, call an emergency medical service or your doctor at once.)*
- poisons including carbon monoxide, chemicals, toxic plants or funguses; overdoses of drugs
- serious illnesses such as heart attack, acute stomach problems, and some kidney or liver disorders
- cancer in various organs, including the lungs *(See a physician for persistent nausea of unknown origin.)*

Phone doctor

Prevention and possible actions: If you feel nauseous and are taking a new medication, call your doctor to review your situation. Many prescription medicines or combinations of drugs have nausea as a side effect. Alternative treatment is often available.

Mild nausea can often be treated with home remedies. Eating something bland often quiets the stomach. Hot tea or a noncarbonated drink may reduce the discomfort, but milk and most carbonated soft drinks can intensify nausea.

Breathing deeply can help control the stomach contractions that come along with nausea and vomiting.

If after trying several home remedies you still feel like throwing up, it may be best to go ahead and vomit. This is especially true if you have a viral disease or a mild case of food poisoning. For many forms of poisoning vomiting is an important first-aid step, but poisoning from harsh chemicals poses special problems, and a stomach pump is much safer than vomiting, which can injure the lining of the digestive system even further.

Phone doctor

Infants and small children often "spit up" or throw up because their stomachs are small and they drink and eat too rapidly. Burping a baby during or after every feeding may prevent some vomiting. If the vomit shoots from the baby's mouth shortly after feeding, it does not indicate a problem unless it happens regularly. If it does happen frequently, see a doctor. *If a baby vomits severely after all feedings in a six-hour period, call your doctor at once.* The baby may have lost a dangerous amount of body fluid.

If you are aiding another person who is vomiting, especially someone who is lying down, help hold the person's head facing down so that the person does not choke.

When nausea persists

Pregnancy often causes "morning sickness." This involves persistent nausea or vomiting every day (often at the same time each day, but not necessarily in the morning) in the first few months of pregnancy. This common symptom is not dangerous—according to some theories, it helps protect the fetus from exposure to harmful substances.

But persistent nausea outside of pregnancy is a symptom of several serious diseases, including cancer, colitis, ulcers, gastroenteritis, and gallstones. These conditions often cause intestinal pain as well.

Persistent nausea after one drink containing alcohol is a sign that the stomach lining is probably inflamed, most likely as a result of alcoholism. Stop drinking, and see a doctor.

Nearsightedness	*See* **Eyes and vision**
Nephritis	*See* **Kidney diseases**

Nerves

BODY SYSTEM

See also
Alcoholism
ALS (amyotrophic lateral sclerosis)
Bell's palsy
Carpal tunnel syndrome
Chicken pox
Cluster headaches
Deafness
Diabetes mellitus, type 1
Diabetes mellitus, type 2
Eyes and vision
Guillain-Barré syndrome
Multiple sclerosis
Myasthenia gravis
Nervous system
Neuralgia
Neuropathy
Numbness
Poliomyelitis ("polio")
Sciatica
Shingles
Tic
Trigeminal neuralgia

Nerve cells, or *neurons,* are the basic building blocks of the nervous system. There are over 200 billion nerve cells in the human body, more than half of them in the brain. These nerve cells enable humans to see, hear, smell, feel, move muscles, think, and experience emotions.

Size and location: Nerve cells are microscopic in diameter, but great concentrations of nerve cells form the *central nervous system* of the brain and spinal cord; the rest combine to form bundles called nerves that extend throughout the body.

The most common nerve cell consists of a rounded cell body and one or more short branchlike filaments, called *dendrites* (DEHN-driytz), that extend out of it. One much longer filament, called an *axon,* also projects out from the cell body, separating into short branches at its tip. Since each axon extends from the central nervous system to the tissue it directs or receives messages from, an axon may be as long as three feet, although most are shorter.

Many longer nerves include not only nerve cells but also other specialized cells that form a sheath of myelin around the axons. This sheath enables messages to travel faster and farther. Nerves may also be surrounded by connective tissue for further protection.

Role: Nerve cells carry messages to and from the brain, making it possible for our central nervous system to do its job. When a nerve cell is stimulated, it produces an electrical impulse that travels outward along its axon, often insulated by a myelin sheath. But the junction between the end of the axon and a dendrite of the next nerve cell, called the *synapse* (SIHN-aaps), is not quite complete. There is a tiny gap, the *synaptic cleft,* between them. In most, but not all, nerve cells the tip of the axon releases chemicals called *neurotransmitters* when stimulated by the electrical impulse. The adjacent dendrite in turn receives the chemical stimulus, and this nerve cell then produces an electrical charge, passing the impulse along to the next nerve cell. In some nerve cells electrical impulses pass directly from one cell to another.

The message passage

Messages travel from one nerve cell to another along fibers called axons that approach, but do not physically touch, the shorter projections called dendrites. The place where an axon conveys its message, a synapse, is where the chemical messengers called neurotransmitters take over.

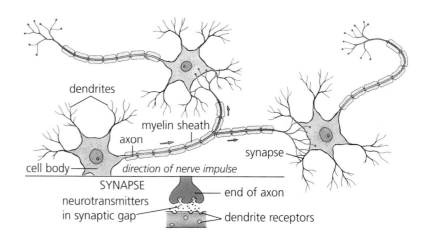

Conditions that affect the nerves: Physical injuries and pressure from tumors can affect nerves and nerve cells in one part of the body, causing numbness, pain, and other problems. Pernicious anemia, poliomyelitis, toxic substances, and infections can also damage nerves. In addition to diseases affecting nerve cells in the brain, various disorders, including ALS (amyotrophic lateral sclerosis) and Guillain-Barré syndrome, damage the nerves themselves. Similar damage to outlying nerves, called neuropathy, often affects those with alcoholism or diabetes mellitus. Diseases that attack the myelin sheath, such as multiple sclerosis, reduce the effectiveness of nerves. Problems with the optic or auditory nerves can cause blindness or deafness. Damage to specific nerves may produce Bell's palsy, a tic in facial or other muscles, or sciatica in the lower back and leg. The chicken pox virus can attack a single nerve also, resulting in shingles.

Nervous system

BODY SYSTEM

After the invention of the microscope physicians and early scientists observed smaller parts of the body, including nerves. But they could not determine how these small parts functioned. Were nerves and muscles physical systems, similar to the mills of the time, with tiny pumps moving fluids through them? Or did the body use chemical processes, a new idea at the time? When electricity became available near the end of the nineteenth century, the idea that nerves work by electricity became popular. Modern scientists, inspired by DNA and computers, find their metaphors for the system in codes and networks.

Today we know that as with the famous blind men analyzing an elephant, each concept told part of the story. The nervous system is a complex network that employs tiny pumps, chemical messengers, electrical transmission, and networks of complex interactions to direct all operations of the body. But the complexity of the nervous system extends far beyond today's understanding of it.

Size and location: While the nervous system is a single, large, interacting system that pervades the body, parts of it occupy specific locations. Because humans are bilaterally symmetrical, the main nerves and collections of nerves come in pairs.

- The brain, for example, is found entirely inside the skull, the main set of bones of the head. The largest part of the brain is a pair of hemispheres that conduct thought and integrate information from the senses.

- Twelve pairs of *cranial nerves* connect directly to the brain. Ten of these pairs travel to parts of the head concerned with sight, sound, smell, and taste, including the *optic nerves* to the eyes and the *auditory nerves* to the ears. The *vagus* (VAY-guhs) *nerves* extend to various organs of the torso, where they control involuntary muscles. The twelfth pair of cranial nerves connects to the shoulder, where they are mostly involved in sense of position for the arms.

- The spinal cord, extending from the brain to the base of the torso and protected by the vertebras, is the main highway for messages to and from the brain. With the brain it forms the *central nervous system.*

- Thirty-two pairs of *spinal nerves* connect to the spinal cord; these are the nerves involved in touch and other sensations, in giving direction to and receiving information from skeletal muscles, and in controlling to some extent the internal organs. For example, the median nerve reaches from the spinal cord to receive messages from and to control the finger muscles.

- Some nerves connected to the cranial and spinal nerves form the *autonomic nervous system.* One set of these nerves handles stress, and another group directly controls most of the organs of the body.

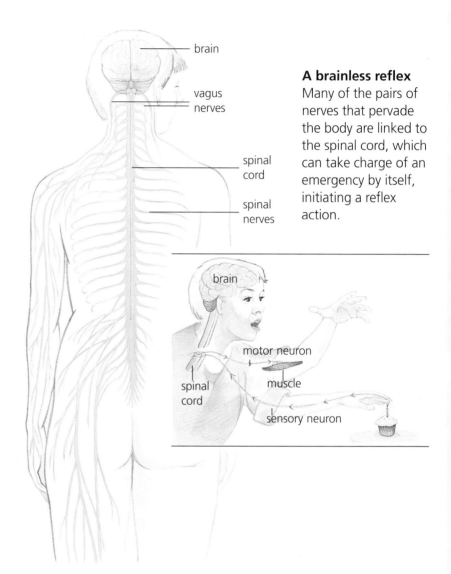

brain

vagus nerves

spinal cord

spinal nerves

A brainless reflex
Many of the pairs of nerves that pervade the body are linked to the spinal cord, which can take charge of an emergency by itself, initiating a reflex action.

brain

motor neuron

muscle

spinal cord

sensory neuron

On the Internet
UNIVERSITY OF WASHINGTON: NEUROSCIENCE FOR KIDS
staff.washington.edu/chudler/ introb.html

Did You Know?

In 1920, Austrian American scientist Otto Loewi proved for the first time that a chemical is produced at the junction between two nerve cells. Today more than 100 chemicals are known to act as neurotransmitters.

Role: Nerves interact with each other in complex and evolving networks by releasing and receiving neurotransmitters on the basis of electrical signals. This system provides us with all our links to the world outside our bodies, integrates the information received, and directs the organs to change in response to the information.

Conditions that affect the nervous system: Many of the diseases that affect the nervous system have their expression in other parts of the body. Conditions that affect the brain, such as alcoholism, Alzheimer's disease, cerebral palsy, and mental illness may produce various physical as well as mental effects. Some infections directly attack the central nervous system, including encephalitis and meningitis. One infection that may strike almost any organ, including the parts of the nervous system, is syphilis.

In a sense, however, all symptomatic diseases attack the nervous system because one would feel no pain or develop no fevers or other observable symptoms without messages passing through the nerves.

Neuralgia

(noo-RAAL-juh)

SYMPTOM

See also
Nerves
Nervous system
Neuropathy
Sciatica
Shingles
Trigeminal neuralgia

On the Internet
VICTORIA DEPARTMENT OF HUMAN SERVICES: BETTER HEALTH CHANNEL (Australia)
www.disability.vic.gov.au/bhcv2/ bhcarticles.nsf/pages/ Neuralgia_explained?open

Neuralgia means "nerve pain." The pain is caused by damage to one or more sensory nerves as a result of disease or injury. Neuralgia is typically a burning, stabbing pain that tends to come and go. Although damage to nerves by cuts, bruises, or other injuries causes immediate and localized pain, this pain is not usually considered neuralgia. Instead, neuralgia usually is pain that appears to have no direct reason for occurring—although in some cases physicians know the cause.

Parts affected: Neuralgia can occur in almost any part of the body, depending on the particular nerve that is damaged.

Related symptoms: Neuropathy may include neuralgic pain among its symptoms, but numbness and other abnormal sensations are more common than pain.

Associations: There are several conditions that cause neuralgia. Two of these are the continuation of chicken pox as shingles, which produces a pain known as *postherpetic neuralgia,* and the specific nerve disorder trigeminal neuralgia. Other neuralgias include the following:

■ *Causalgia* (kawz-AL-juh, or "burning pain") and *reflex sympathetic dystrophy* are related disorders caused by mechanical damage to sensory nerves, usually as a result of accident or violence. Causalgia was first identified among wounded soldiers during the Civil War. Damaged nerves normally become less and less painful as they heal. But sometimes, for reasons that are not understood, the nerves become *hypersensitive:* Even the mildest kind of stimulus, such as a light touch or a change in temperature, may trigger severe pain.
■ *Stump* and *phantom-limb pain* may appear after the amputa-

tion of an arm or leg. Severed sensory nerves normally transmit less and less pain as a wound heals, but in rare instances an area of amputation remains painful (stump pain), or else pain is "felt" in the area where the severed limb used to be (phantom-limb pain).

Relief of symptoms: Mild neuralgia is treated with painkillers such as aspirin or ibuprofen. Other medications, such as corticosteroids and antidepressants, may give relief in more severe cases.

Severe neuralgias may be treated with *nerve blocks*. Short-term nerve blocks are achieved using injections of local anesthetics to temporarily stop the transmission of pain messages; long-term blocks are accomplished by surgically cutting a sensory nerve or destroying the nerve with chemicals.

Neural tube defects

DISEASE

TYPE: DEVELOPMENTAL

On the Internet
MEDLINE PLUS
www.nlm.nih.gov/medlineplus/
neuraltubedefects.html

The nervous system of a human embryo starts to form within the first month of pregnancy. It begins with a flattened layer of cells known as the *neural plate*. The sides of the plate curl toward each other and join, forming a *neural tube* from which the brain and spinal cord develop.

Sometimes this process goes wrong, and the tube fails to close at some point along its length. The result is a neural tube defect. Muscle and bone, which would normally develop to protect the nerve tissue, cannot grow across such a gap. An opening in the part of the neural tube destined to become the spinal cord causes spina bifida (SPIY-nuh BIHF-ih-duh). A gap at the end that will become the brain results in either *encephalocele* (ehn-SEHF-uh-luh-SEEL) or *anencephaly* (AAN-uhn-SEHF-uh-lee). Neural tube defects may be the cause of some cases of hydrocephalus.

Encephalocele (literally "bulging of the brain") is an opening in the skull through which the brain membranes or even part of the brain itself can bulge outward. Anencephaly ("absence of brain") is a fatal condition in which both the back of the skull and part of the brain are missing.

Cause: The causes of neural tube defects are unknown. They may be partly genetic, for they tend to run in families and are concentrated in certain ethnic groups. There is good evidence that a diet low in the B vitamin folate (folic acid) contributes to these defects. But they also occur more often than usual in children of mothers who have diabetes mellitus, who have had a high fever during early pregnancy, or who take the drugs valproic acid or carbamazepine for epilepsy.

Incidence: Anencephaly affects fewer than 1 in 10,000 live births. Encephalocele occurs in about 1 in 10,000 births. In addition, many affected fetuses are miscarried or stillborn.

Noticeable symptoms: Serious neural tube defects are evident at birth.

Diagnosis: A standard test of the mother's blood during pregnancy may reveal a chemical produced by the nervous system of the fetus. The presence of this chemical indicates that the fetus has an open neural tube defect from which the chemical has leaked out. Neural tube defects may also be visible by ultrasound examination during pregnancy.

Treatment options: Spina bifida and encephalocele can be repaired surgically, but the brain or the spinal cord may be permanently damaged.

Outlook: The outlook varies widely. Anencephaly is quickly fatal. Encephalocele is likely to involve severe brain damage, especially if brain tissue protrudes through the opening in the skull.

Prevention: The vitamin folate appears to reduce by 50 to 70% the risk of neural tube defects. Since half of American pregnancies are unexpected, a minimum dose of 400 micrograms (0.4 milligrams) a day is recommended for all women of childbearing age, and 800 micrograms a day for those who are either pregnant or intending to become so. Women who are considered at especially high risk, such as mothers of affected children, are urged to take 4,000 micrograms, or 4 milligrams, daily.

To aid in the prevention of neural tube defects, a synthetic form of folate, folic acid, is now added to processed grain products in the United States. Some fortified breakfast cereals contain a full 400 micrograms per serving. For higher doses folic acid tablets are readily available.

Neuropathy

(noo-ROP-uh-thee)

SYMPTOM

See also
Alcoholism
Anemias
Diabetes mellitus, type 1
Diabetes mellitus, type 2
Lead poisoning
Nervous system
Neuralgia
Poisoning
Vitamin-deficiency diseases

On the Internet
MAYO CLINIC
www.mayoclinic.com/health/
peripheral-neuropathy/DS00131

The peripheral nerves are those in the body outside the central nervous system (the brain and spinal cord). When peripheral nerves become damaged for some reason, one symptom may be neuropathy ("nerve disease"). The first signs are usually tingling or other abnormal sensations in the skin. Numbness and muscle weakness are likely to follow. Eventually, the muscles may atrophy, or waste away, from lack of proper use.

Neuropathy is sometimes called *peripheral neuropathy* and sometimes referred to as *neuritis,* or inflammation of the nerves. Either or both of the two main kinds of peripheral nerves may be affected: the sensory nerves, which register sensations such as touch and temperature, or the motor nerves, which control muscle activity.

Parts affected: The signs of neuropathy usually appear first in the hands and feet. They then spread through the arms and legs to the rest of the body.

Related symptoms: The tingling feeling of a foot or hand "falling asleep" after being in the same position or after having something press on a leg or an arm is a mild form of neuropathy. When the blood supply to a nerve is cut off by body position or pressure, the nerve reacts with distress. The distress goes away when movement restores normal blood flow.

The numbness and weakness of neuropathy are sometimes accompanied by attacks of the burning, stabbing pain called neuralgia.

Associations: The damage to the peripheral nerves is most often caused by either diabetes mellitus or alcoholism. It can also result from kidney failure, from vitamin-deficiency diseases such as pernicious anemia (vitamin B_{12} deficiency), or from poisoning by substances such as mercury, lead, carbon monoxide, or the pesticides called organophosphates (such as DDT and dieldrin).

Hereditary neuropathies are classified as *Charcot-Marie-Tooth disease,* named for the three doctors who first discovered the disease in 1886.

Prevention and possible actions: Neuropathy can often be prevented, or its progress slowed, by treating the underlying cause, such as diabetes, alcoholism, kidney failure, nutritional deficiency, poisoning, and so forth.

Relief of symptoms: Other than physical therapy to cope with the loss of mobility, there is no specific treatment for the numbness and muscle weakness of neuropathy.

Neutropenia

(NOO-truh-PEE-nee-uh)

DISEASE

TYPE: CHEMICAL; GENETIC

See also
Blood
Cancers
Immune system
Lymphocytes

On the Internet
MERCK MANUAL:
HOME EDITION
www.merck.com/mmhe/sec14/
ch174/ch174b.html

Phone doctor

The bone marrow produces various types of white blood cells. The most numerous are *neutrophils*, mobile cells filled with evenly distributed granules, that are the body's first defense against infection. A significant decrease in the number of neutrophils is known as neutropenia, or *granulocytopenia* (GRAAN-yuh-loh-SIYT-uh-PEE-nee-uh). Complete loss of neutrophils is called *agranulocytosis* (ay-GRAAN-yuh-loh-siy-TOH-sihs).

Cause: Neutropenia is a rare disorder that is usually caused by exposure to medications that suppress the production of neutrophils. Cancer chemotherapy is the most common cause of neutropenia. Drugs such as penicillins, sulfonamides, phenothiazines, antithyroids, and anticonvulsants sometimes also reduce the number of neutrophils in the blood. The antipsychotic drug clozapine (trade name: Clozaril) may cause life-threatening neutropenia, so people taking this drug must have their blood closely monitored. Exposure to industrial chemicals such as solvents and hydrocarbons may cause neutropenia as well. In some cases, such as infantile genetic neutropenia, the disease is hereditary.

Noticeable symptoms: A reduced neutrophil count increases susceptibility to infections. Fever, sore throat, and mouth and throat ulcers may be signs of neutropenia. *See a doctor if you experience severe infections or if you have one infection after another.* Tell the doctor what medications you have been taking, particularly if you believe that they may be related to the problem.

Diagnosis: If the doctor suspects neutropenia, a blood sample will be taken and sent to a laboratory, where a count of neutrophils in the sample will be made. If the neutrophil level is low, a doctor will perform a bone marrow aspiration and biopsy. In this procedure a small amount of marrow is removed and examined. The biopsy helps the doctor make a precise diagnosis of the disease and its cause.

Treatment options: If neutropenia is caused by a medication or other chemical, exposure to that chemical will be eliminated. If a severe infection is the cause of neutropenia, the patient may be hospitalized and treated with antibiotics. Several medicines can stimulate the growth of neutrophils, such as sargramostim (Leukine), filgrastim (Neupogen), and pegfilgrastim (Neulasta).

Stages and progress: It is important to treat neutropenia as early as possible. Left untreated, it can make a person susceptible to severe illnesses such as bacterial pneumonia and septic shock. With treatment neutropenia often clears up in several weeks.

Neutrophils

See **Phagocytes and other leukocytes**

Nose and throat conditions

REFERENCE

Did You Know?
A physician who treats nose and throat conditions is an otolaryngologist (OH-toh-lahr-ihng-GOL-uh-jihst).

Although they have separate openings to the outside world, the nose and throat connect at the back of the throat. Physicians who specialize in treating conditions that affect one also treat the other.

Several other parts of the body connect at or near the junction of nose and throat (also called the *pharynx*). The *sinuses* are air-filled cavities in the skull that are connected to the nose. The *esophagus* joins the throat to the rest of the digestive system, while the *trachea* connects the nose to the respiratory system via the throat. A flap called the *epiglottis* closes the top of the trachea when food or water is being swallowed; it opens to permit air to enter the trachea. Thus the throat acts as a complex gateway.

Role: The nose is a sense organ, with a direct connection to a part of the brain that is involved with deep emotions instead of thought. Although the throat itself is not a sense organ, it participates with the tongue and nose in the sense of taste.

In addition to being an organ of smell, the nose is the place best designed to admit air into the body, for it can warm and moisten it, and its hairs can filter out dust. Often there is a need for more air than can pass through the nose, however, and the mouth is used as a supplemental way to take it in. From either the nose or the mouth air then passes through the throat.

Gargle saltwater

Phone doctor

Food that approaches the throat is sampled in various ways. Although the actual taste receptors, called *taste buds,* are on the tongue, they can sense only four or five different flavors—sweet, salt, bitter, sour, and perhaps the taste of monosodium glutamate. The rest of taste consists of odors sampled by the nose and texture and warmth felt by various parts of the mouth.

Conditions that affect the nose: The center section of the nose, between the two nostrils, is called the *septum.* If it is congenitally shifted to one side, or if it becomes shifted as a result of injury, it is said to be *deviated.* Deviated septum, which can usually be corrected by surgery, interferes with normal breathing and causes nasal passages to block more readily.

Sometimes the mucous membrane can thicken and protrude into the air passages. Such a projection, called a *polyp,* can also block nasal passages. Near the place where the nasal passages join the throat, lymphatic tissue forms two bodies called *adenoids* (AAD-n-oidz). Sometimes in children the adenoids become frequently infected or block the airways and must be removed surgically.

The medical term for inability to smell is *anosmia* (aan-OZ-mee-uh). Usually, anosmia is temporary, caused by blocked nasal passages as a result of a common cold or allergies. In some individuals anosmia is permanent or long-lasting. Injury can affect the part of the brain connected with smell, known as the olfactory center, for example. Sometimes drinking alcohol on a daily basis has anosmia as one result.

Conditions that affect the throat: *Pharyngitis* (FAAR-ihn-JIY-tihs) is the medical term for "sore throat." For many people all the air that is breathed travels through the nostrils (the outside openings of the nose); for others the nostrils seem too small for this purpose. People who are regular mouth breathers are more likely to develop pharyngitis. Often physicians suggest gargling with a salt solution to alleviate minor pharyngitis.

Viruses cause most pharyngitis, but most serious forms result from such bacteria as "strep" and *Hemophilus influenzae,* type B. Bacterial infections of the throat can affect the heart or other organs if not halted with antibiotics. ***A sore throat that persists for more than a week or that seems unusually severe is possibly bacterial and requires medical attention.***

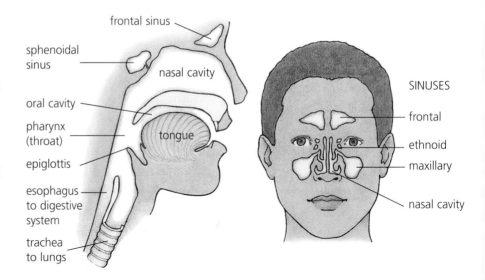

frontal sinus

sphenoidal sinus

nasal cavity

oral cavity

pharynx (throat)

tongue

epiglottis

esophagus to digestive system

trachea to lungs

SINUSES

frontal

ethnoid

maxillary

nasal cavity

The passages for the respiratory system and digestive system connect at the back of the throat, where the epiglottis acts as gatekeeper. Also connected to the nose and throat are the openings to the skull called sinuses.

Emergency Room

In young children a bacterial infection can produce *epiglottitis* (EHP-ih-glot-TIY-tihs), inflammation of the epiglottis. This requires immediate attention, especially if the airway begins to shut down completely.

Sometimes liquid nasal mucus that overflows the sinuses or that comes directly from the lining of the nose irritates glands at the back of the throat, a condition called *postnasal drip*. This can result in unpleasant breath and a bad taste in the back of the mouth. Postnasal drip can often be controlled with decongestants or antihistamines. Surgery may be needed to correct especially bad cases.

The back of the throat contains several masses of lymphatic tissue known as the *tonsils*. Like all lymphatic tissue, the tonsils help filter germs from the system and can be infected by the concentrations thus produced. This may result in the inflammation tonsillitis.

Associations: Nearly all the minor viral diseases that have flu-like symptoms, from the common cold to an unspecified "virus," cause the mucous membranes of the nose to swell and release watery mucus; they may also cause pharyngitis. Allergies, especially hay fever, produce similar symptoms. Among the many minor problems that affect the mouth and throat are cankers and cold sores. Cough is a symptom that also arises in and can affect the throat.

Avoid alcohol

Phone doctor

Don't smoke

Various more serious infections can settle in the nose or throat, including diphtheria, influenza, leprosy, measles, pertussis, syphilis, and typhoid fever.

Heavy use of alcohol or tobacco is the source of most cancers of the throat and mouth, but cancers of the sinuses or nasal passages can arise spontaneously. Any unexplained obstruction of the nasal passages or bulging or numbness of the face should be examined by a physician.

Nosebleed

SYMPTOM

Although there are many folk remedies for nosebleed, nothing works as well as simply standing for several minutes with the head thrown back as you pinch closed the fleshy tip of the nose. During this time you need to breathe through your mouth.

Most everyone experiences nosebleed—also called *epistaxis* (EHP-ih-STAAK-sihs)—at some point in his or her life. Membranes inside the nose are delicate and contain blood vessels that are easily damaged. Such damage often results in blood streaming from the nostrils. Except for cases of persistent or repeated bleeding, nosebleed seldom is a cause for concern.

Parts affected: For young people membranes at the front of the nose are most often involved. Usually, the broken blood vessel is in the front part of the septum, the cartilage separating the two nasal cavities. With older people, however, the bleeding sometimes comes from farther back in the nose. These nosebleeds can be harder to treat.

Related symptoms: If a hard blow to the nose has caused the bleeding, there may be some additional soreness or bruising associated with the injury. Colds, sinusitis, and allergies each bring on their set of symptoms, such as headache, runny nose, and sneezing, and sometimes bleeding from the nose.

Associations: In addition to allergies, colds, and sinus infections, more serious conditions can also cause nosebleed, such as a tumor toward the back of the nose. Hypertension or alcoholism may be responsible for frequent episodes of nosebleed with no apparent cause. Bleeding from the nose is one of the symptoms of a fractured skull. People who use cocaine sometimes damage the lining of the nose; this can result in bleeding as well as other symptoms.

Radiation therapy, chemotherapy for cancer, and various powerful medicines may destroy blood platelets, producing a tendency to bleed more readily. This also may result in nosebleed.

Phone doctor

See also
Allergies
Blood
Common cold
Drug abuse
Hay fever
Head injuries
Hemophilias
Hypertension
Nose and throat conditions
Sneezing

Emergency Room

Some people fear anemia from prolonged or repeated nosebleed, but this is unlikely as usually very little blood is lost, even though it may seem like a large amount.

Prevention and possible actions: For most people nosebleed happens only at infrequent intervals and clears up quickly. If bleeding occurs often, or if there is difficulty in stopping it, get medical help.

Where no serious underlying problem is involved, there are some steps that speed healing and reduce the chances of getting new nosebleeds. A person should refrain from blowing the nose for about a dozen hours after having a nosebleed. The change in air pressure may restart bleeding. Use of a vaporizer or humidifier helps keep nasal passages from drying out. Do not pick the nose. Putting petroleum jelly on the nasal septum one or two times a day may also help prevent new bleeding.

Relief of symptoms: Bleeding from the nose usually can be stopped quickly with the following procedure:

- Sit or stand with your head tilted slightly back. Do not lie down; it increases pressure in the blood vessels of the nose.
- While sitting or standing, gently pinch the nose closed with your fingers. Apply pressure on the front, fleshy part of the nose. This should slow the blood flow from the broken vessel and help formation of a blood clot.
- Breathe through your mouth, and hold the nose closed for about five or ten minutes.
- If bleeding starts again, repeat the procedure. But if bleeding persists after a couple of tries, see your physician, or go to a medical emergency center.

At a medical center treatment may involve nothing more than insertion of a medicated cotton ball in the nasal passageway to help promote healing. Cauterizing the broken blood vessel may be necessary if bleeding persists, however. In this procedure a physician desensitizes the inside of the nose with a topical anesthetic and then burns the broken vessel with a chemical agent or with a special instrument. The nostril may then be packed with gauze for several days to further promote healing.

Bleeding from the back of the nose is much harder to stop and often must be treated by a nose-and-throat specialist. If blood is draining into the throat from the back of the nose, more blood may be lost than the patient realizes. This kind of nosebleed can be life-threatening when not treated.

Nosocomial infections

(NOHS-oh-KOH-mee-uhl)

REFERENCE

See also
Bacteria and disease
Bedsores
"Staph"
Viruses and disease
Wounds

Each year nearly 40 million people are admitted to a hospital in the United States. About 2 million of these patients get more than treatment for their medical condition; they also acquire a serious bacterial infection. For tens of thousands of these people their health is so fragile and the infection so severe that they die.

Infections transmitted to people while hospitalized are called nosocomial infections (*nosocomium* is Latin for "hospital"). Nosocomial infections are sometimes called *hospital-acquired infections.*

Many nosocomial infections are associated with medical procedures that break the barrier of the skin or that place a medical device into the body. Such procedures include surgery, catheterization (placing a tube into the urethra to drain urine from the bladder), and ventilation (running a tube connected to an oxygen supply into the lungs to help the patient breathe). Catheters or ventilators may remain in place for days, weeks, or occasionally months.

The risk for nosocomial infections is higher in some areas of hospitals than in others and for some groups of patients than others. Simple treatment in a hospital emergency room or outpatient clinic is not likely to result in a nosocomial infection. The intensive care unit (ICU), on the other hand, carries a higher risk for nosocomial infection. Patients in an ICU tend to be very ill, be hospitalized for long periods of time, and have more procedures that put them at risk.

Cause: Many patients come into a hospital to be treated for a serious infection. Some are ill from other causes, but also carry dangerous bacteria. When these patients receive treatment, harmful bacteria may contaminate instruments, devices, or the hands and clothing of the people who are caring for them. If instruments or devices are not sterilized properly before they are used on another patient, they can transfer the bacteria. If the medical staff does not follow proper procedures for hand washing and changing of gowns and gloves, they can transfer the bacteria on their bodies and infect patients.

Prevention by institutions: Hospitals can take many steps to reduce the number of nosocomial infections in their patients.

■ Disposable instruments and devices, used with only one patient, reduce infections.

■ Thorough sterilization of instruments and devices that are reused is absolutely necessary.

■ Laparoscopes and endoscopes, devices that allow surgery to be performed through a tiny incision rather than a large one, reduce nosocomial infections related to surgical procedures.

■ But possibly the most important step is to provide good infection-control training to all staff. This includes training staff who have contact with patients to wear gowns and gloves when performing any procedure that might result in the transfer of bacteria and then to dispose of gowns and gloves properly. It also includes repeated training in proper and frequent hand washing since contaminated hands may be the major way bacteria are transferred from one patient to another.

A more expensive and difficult step is to try to identify every patient with an infection. This involves screening everyone admitted to a hospital to identify carriers who have dangerous bacteria in their bodies but are not ill from the bacteria. Such carriers would then be treated with the same precautions to control the infection as patients who are ill with serious infections.

Prevention for patients: There are steps a patient can take to reduce his or her risk of a nosocomial infection. Ask about the rate of hospital-acquired infections at the hospital where treatment will occur. Find out which devices will be used for treatment and whether disposable versions are available. Ask about hospital rules about hand washing and other measures to control infections. And, to protect other patients, be sure to report any known infections or history of infections when the medical history is taken.

Numbness

SYMPTOM

You have probably heard people say "my foot fell asleep," or "I feel pins and needles." Maybe you have even used one of these expressions yourself. If so, you are describing a common sign of numbness, or loss of feeling in part of the body.

Parts affected: Numbness often occurs, along with a tingling feeling, when you momentarily "pinch a nerve" (deprive a nerve of its blood supply for a time) in an arm, leg, hand, or foot. This generally happens after you have been in one position for a long time, perhaps sitting or sleeping. The feeling disappears shortly after changing position. Numbness in extremities, especially fingers or toes, may stem from frostbite. Numbness in a part of the head, neck, or trunk is more likely to have a serious origin.

Related symptoms: Sometimes numbness is associated with a stiff neck, pains in the hand or arm, difficulty in speaking, blurred vision, dementia, dizziness, or weakness in a part of the body. Each of these symptoms, especially when combined with numbness or with each other, indicates a disease that requires medical attention.

A different effect of keeping a part of the body in the same position is cramp, a sharp pain caused by muscle contractions.

Associations: Arthritis or injury to the neck can result in a pinched nerve. This in turn can cause numbness or tingling sensations in the arm or hand, usually along with pain on one side of the neck. Another condition causing similar numbness and stiff neck, especially in older people, is *spondylosis*.

Numbness in the fingers, hand, or arm may be a sign of carpal tunnel syndrome. It is also associated with Raynaud's disease, a disorder of the blood vessels that often produces numbness in the fingers or toes.

Any sudden, unexplained numbness should be checked by medical professionals as soon as possible. Numbness combined with blurred vision, mental confusion, or dizziness may be a sign of a small stroke, called a TIA (transient ischemic attack), which often precedes a major stroke. Stroke can often be prevented, and the damage from a stroke can be minimized if it is dealt with quickly.

Numbness along with difficulty in speaking or weakness or paralysis in the arms or legs may be a symptom of a major stroke. ***Get emergency help at once if these symptoms occur.***

Numbness is also associated with neuropathy caused by alcoholism, arthritis, diabetes mellitus, Hodgkin's disease, lymphoma, multiple sclerosis, and other diseases that affect nerves. In these instances other symptoms of the disease usually precede numbness, sometimes by many years.

Call ambulance

Prevention and possible actions: If you have a problem with your limbs "falling asleep," take the following precautions:

■ Stop smoking. Smoking slows blood circulation, which in turn makes numbness in the limbs more likely.

■ If you do a lot of repetitive tasks with your hands, such as typing, hammering, or piano playing, take a break every half hour, and gently rotate your wrists a few times to prevent carpal tunnel syndrome.

The numbness of a TIA is often a result of hypertension, and TIA can frequently be prevented by getting blood pressure under control. Physicians may also prescribe small doses of aspirin or a blood thinner to persons thought to be susceptible to stroke after a TIA.

Relief of symptoms: Numbness that does not disappear after moving the affected part can sometimes be helped by gently massaging the affected area. If numbness persists for several hours or more, it may be a symptom of a disease that requires medical attention.

Don't smoke

Phone doctor

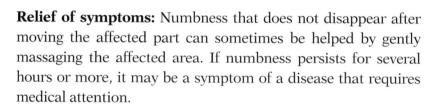

Obesity

DISEASE

TYPE: GENETIC; HORMONAL; LIFESTYLE

Obesity is more than simply being a bit overweight. Increasingly, physicians and public health officials define obesity as a disease in itself—one that increases the risk of other diseases. Complications of obesity include higher risk of diabetes mellitus, hypertension (high blood pressure), stroke, heart disease, gallbladder problems, kidney disorders, gout, osteoarthritis, certain cancers, and complications during pregnancy. Each year, more than 300,000 deaths in the United States alone are linked to obesity.

The more overweight the individual, the greater the risk. People who are 20 to 30% heavier than their optimal weight, for example, are three times as likely to die of diabetes mellitus. Someone who is 40% or more overweight doubles the risk of dying from heart disease. Risks are present among children as

On the Internet

AMERICAN OBESITY
ASSOCIATION
www.obesity.org/subs/fastfacts/
aoafactsheets.shtml

CENTERS FOR DISEASE CONTROL
AND PREVENTION (CDC):
BMI for Children and Teens
www.cdc.gov/nccdphp/dnpa/
bmi/bmi-for-age.htm

well as adults; for instance, obese children are twice as likely to have diabetes as are children of normal weight.

Cause: Eating excessive amounts of food and living a sedentary life are the main causes of obesity. If you consume more calories than your body uses, you gain weight. Certain eating trends play a role in increased calorie consumption, including large portion sizes and a preference for fast foods and convenience foods (usually high in fat, sugar, and calories) and sugary drinks.

Genetics also plays a role in obesity, in ways that are not yet totally clear. In some rare disorders, such as Bardet-Biedl syndrome and Prader-Willi syndrome, genes directly cause obesity. In the broader population, however, it may be that a variety of genes increase susceptibility to obesity. For instance, genes can influence appetite, how the body stores fat, and how it burns calories for energy.

Some illnesses may cause weight gain and lead to obesity. These include polycystic ovary syndrome, in which ovaries produce cysts instead of eggs, and Cushing's disease, caused by overproduction of an adrenal gland hormone. Certain drugs, including steroids and some antidepressants, may also cause weight gain.

Incidence: Obesity rates are rising sharply, with an estimated 1 billion obese people worldwide, including 22 million children. In the United States, about 31% of people age 20 or older and 16% of youths age 6 to 19 are obese—rates matched and in some cases exceeded in other countries. Percentages of overweight people also are rising, including among the young. Public health officials estimate that if present trends continue, nearly 50% of children in the Americas and about 38% of children in the European Union will be overweight by 2010.

Diagnosis: Doctors use a measure called the body mass index (BMI) to define obesity. Officially, BMI is weight in kilograms divided by the square of height in meters. This measure can be translated into U.S. customary measures based on pounds and inches. A healthy BMI for most adults is between 18.5 and 24.9. A BMI of 25 to 29.9 is considered overweight. One of 30 or higher is considered obese. For children and teens, BMI ranges take into account normal differences in body fat between boys and girls, as well as differences in body fat at various ages.

A large waist circumference is another sign of obesity. A

waist of more than 40 inches around for adult men or 35 inches for adult women indicates excess abdominal fat. Health risks are highest for persons with a waist-to-hips ratio greater than 1.

The doctor will also review the patient's medical history, paying particular attention to behaviors such as smoking and high stress levels, which in combination with excess weight can heighten health risks.

Treatment options: The first line of treatment is to alter the person's energy intake and expenditure. A seemingly infinite array of diet plans is available, but obese persons require a plan that can be maintained for the long term, even for life. A reasonable goal might be to lose one to two pounds a week. This can be accomplished by eating less at meals and exercising more, so that the body is burning about 500 to 750 more calories than it is getting each day. Also, health guidelines stress the importance of a balanced diet, keeping fats below 30% of total calories.

People who have problems shedding pounds may find that joining a weight-loss group can provide the motivation they need to succeed. Most such groups also educate members in what constitutes a sensible diet.

Should self-help measures fail, the doctor may prescribe medication. The history of medications for weight loss suggests caution because of side effects such as higher heart rate and blood pressure. Also, research shows that obese people who take drugs alone lose much less weight than people who also adopt a program of healthy eating and exercise.

For people with severe obesity or with serious weight-related illnesses such as diabetes or heart disease, bariatric surgery may be recommended. Such surgery aids weight loss by restricting the amount of food a person is able to consume and, in some operations, reducing the amount of calories that the body can absorb from the small intestine. One commonly used procedure is gastric banding, in which the surgeon places a band around the upper part of the stomach, sealing off most of the stomach and thus reducing the amount of food it can hold. Long-term success in losing and keeping off weight, however, depends on patients' willingness to adopt healthy eating behaviors and regular physical activity.

Eat low-fat foods

12-Step meeting

How to determine your BMI

BMI	19	20	21	22	23	24	25	26	27	28	29	30	31	32	33	34	35
Height (inches)	Body Weight (pounds)																
58	91	96	100	105	110	115	119	124	129	134	138	143	148	153	158	162	167
59	94	99	104	109	114	119	124	128	133	138	143	148	153	158	163	168	173
60	97	102	107	112	118	123	128	133	138	143	148	153	158	163	168	174	179
61	100	106	111	116	122	127	132	137	143	148	153	158	164	169	174	180	185
62	104	109	115	120	126	131	136	142	147	153	158	164	169	175	180	186	191
63	107	113	118	124	130	135	141	146	152	158	163	169	175	180	186	191	197
64	110	116	122	128	134	140	145	151	157	163	169	174	180	186	192	197	204
65	114	120	126	132	138	144	150	156	162	168	174	180	186	192	198	204	210
66	118	124	130	136	142	148	155	161	167	173	179	186	192	198	204	210	216
67	121	127	134	140	146	153	159	166	172	178	185	191	198	204	211	217	223
68	125	131	138	144	151	158	164	171	177	184	190	197	203	210	216	223	230
69	128	135	142	149	155	162	169	176	182	189	196	203	209	216	223	230	236
70	132	139	146	153	160	167	174	181	188	195	202	209	216	222	229	236	243
71	136	143	150	157	165	172	179	186	193	200	208	215	222	229	236	243	250
72	140	147	154	162	169	177	184	191	199	206	213	221	228	235	242	250	258
73	144	151	159	166	174	182	189	197	204	212	219	227	235	242	250	257	265
74	148	155	163	171	179	186	194	202	210	218	225	233	241	249	256	264	272
75	152	160	168	176	184	192	200	208	216	224	232	240	248	256	264	272	279
76	156	164	172	180	189	197	205	213	221	230	238	246	254	263	271	279	287

Exercise

Prevention: Checking weight on a regular basis, such as weekly or monthly, is useful, since changes can provide an early warning that you are gaining. It is much easier to modify your diet or increase your amount of exercise before you are significantly overweight. Maintaining a regular exercise program that includes at minimum three periods lasting at least half an hour, in addition to eating moderately, is the most important preventive habit.

Obsessive-compulsive disorder

DISEASE

TYPE: MENTAL

See also
Asperger's syndrome
Autism
Brain
Clinical depression
Mental illnesses
Schizophrenia
Stress
Tourette's syndrome

On the Internet
NATIONAL INSTITUTE
OF MENTAL HEALTH
www.nimh.nih.gov/
HealthInformation/ocdmenu.cfm

Obsessive-compulsive disorder (OCD) is characterized by ongoing bouts with obsessions (persistent involuntary thoughts or urges) and compulsions (persistent ritualistic behaviors). The obsessions and compulsions distress the patient, but they cannot be controlled and interfere with the patient's normal life.

Cause: The cause of OCD is not known, though genetic factors are believed to increase risk. Brain-imaging studies suggest that OCD patients have unique patterns of brain activity; in particular, the brain neurotransmitter called serotonin appears to have a role. Some cases of OCD have occurred in children and young adults following infections with certain streptococcus bacteria or herpes viruses.

Upbringing—for instance, excessive parental emphasis on cleanliness and hand washing—is not believed to be a cause of OCD. Nor does stress appear to cause OCD, but OCD symptoms can worsen with stress.

Incidence: OCD was once thought to be relatively rare, but improved education of patients and healthcare providers has increased identification of individuals with the disease. OCD affects 2 to 3% of people, or about 7 million Americans. Studies indicate a similar incidence worldwide. Symptoms usually become apparent between the ages of 20 and 30; 75% of those who develop OCD show symptoms by age 30.

Noticeable symptoms: Psychological studies have shown that most people at one time or another have obsessive thoughts or engage in compulsive behavior patterns. But people with OCD suffer these uncontrollable episodes over and over again.

As the name of the disorder suggests, there are both obsessions and compulsions to contend with.

Obsessions: These may take the form of images, such as mental scenes involving violence, aggression, or sex. Or they may be fears about such things as disease, contamination, or seemingly remote dangers, such as being cut with a knife.

There may also be urges, such as the urge to shout out obscenities. An urge is considered a special kind of obsession, since the behavior may be controlled even if the thoughts cannot be.

Compulsions: These usually involve actions. The two most common compulsions are *washing* and *checking*. Washing is an extension of an obsession with cleanliness, while checking is an extension of worrying over details. In both cases the behaviors are ritualistic and performed over and over again according to the patient's rules. For example, an OCD patient might check the stove ten times before leaving the house to prevent an accidental fire. Other typical checking behaviors include repeatedly trying doors to make sure they are locked or checking to make sure faucets are turned off.

Among other typical rituals associated with OCD are hoarding, counting, and excessive organizing.

Diagnosis: A thorough psychiatric examination is done. Coupled with the patient's awareness of his or her obsessions, this often makes diagnosis straightforward. However, OCD patients sometimes have additional psychiatric illnesses such as Tourette's syndrome, depression, attention deficit disorder, eating disorders, or substance abuse, which can make diagnosis more difficult.

Treatment options: Treatment, undertaken with a psychologist or psychotherapist, generally includes a combination of behavior therapy and medications. During therapy, patients learn how to control their anxiety without engaging in compulsive behavior. They may also be taught relaxation techniques that help relieve symptoms. Gradually, patients are able to lengthen the period of time during which they can behave normally, even in stressful circumstances.

Antidepressant medications that influence serotonin levels, such as Prozac, may be prescribed. If this is not effective, a tricyclic antidepressant called clomipramine may be tried. In some cases, both drugs are prescribed.

Onychomycosis

See **Finger and toenail fungus**

Opportunistic diseases

REFERENCE

Healthy people have many different kinds of microorganisms living on their bodies and inside their bodies. Normally, these organisms do not cause problems. Their numbers are kept small by good hygiene—bathing washes thousands of microorganisms off the skin—and by cells of the immune system. If populations of the microorganisms inside the body grow too large, the immune system cells destroy extra microorganisms. This process keeps a balance that allows the microorganisms to live in harmony with the body. The immune system also regularly checks the body for precancerous cells and destroys them before they become malignant.

People with damaged immune systems may lack the white blood cells that control the size of the population of certain microorganisms and that recognize certain kinds of precancerous cells. As a result the microorganisms can grow out of control and cause diseases, and precancerous cells can grow into cancers. These diseases are called opportunistic because microorganisms and precancerous cells take the opportunity of a weakened immune system to grow out of control and harm the body.

Immune system deficiencies: Opportunistic diseases are commonly thought of in reference to AIDS, but these diseases can occur in people with any condition that seriously damages their immune system. This includes people born with immune system disorders and people who have had organ transplants. (Recipients of organ transplants take medicine every day to depress their immune system. This is so the immune system does not attack the transplanted organ and cause it to fail.) Since opportunistic diseases are usually the cause of death of people with AIDS, much research has been done on opportunistic diseases associated with AIDS.

Among the frail elderly there is often a decline in immune function. These individuals, like younger people with damaged immune systems, are especially vulnerable to certain infections. Episodes of food poisoning in nursing homes can quickly cause deaths if the infected individuals are not treated quickly.

Diseases: Opportunistic diseases can occur in many parts of the body: *Pneumocystis carinii* pneumonia (PCP) is a disease of the lungs; cryptosporidiosis affects the intestines, preventing absorption of food; *cytomegalovirus* attacks the eyes and can lead to blindness; and *Kaposi's sarcoma* is a cancer of the blood vessels. These are all diseases that are frequently seen in people with HIV infection. Parasites are often opportunistic as well.

People with organ transplants often develop a variety of cancers because their immune systems are artificially depressed with medicine.

Tuberculosis is opportunistic with respect to the immune system and also attacks people with poor nutrition or other weaknesses.

Organ transplants

REFERENCE

See also
Lymphocytes

On the Internet
DEPARTMENT OF HEALTH
AND HUMAN SERVICES
www.organdonor.gov

> **Did You Know?**
> People indicate their desire to donate organs and tissues by signing Uniform Donor Cards. They tell their family about this decision so that their wishes will be honored at the time of death.

Thousands of people whose kidneys are diseased, hearts are failing, or livers are damaged are enjoying prolonged lives thanks to transplantation, a surgical technique that implants organs or tissues from one human body into another. Many additional people could benefit from the procedure if there were sufficient donors.

Several types of transplants are possible. An *autograft* is the transplant of tissue from one part of a person's body to another, such as a skin graft in a burn victim. An *allograft*—the most common type of transplant surgery—is an organ or tissue transplanted from one human (usually deceased) to another. A *xenograft* is a transplant from one species to another, such as a pig heart valve into a human.

Cause: The first successful transplant of a vital organ was the transplant of a kidney between identical twins in 1954. Since then, transplants of hearts, lungs, livers, pancreases, and intestines have become commonplace. Each day in the United States, about 74 people receive an organ transplant.

In addition to organs, surgeons transplant tissues such as bone, bone marrow, blood vessels, skin, and cornea (the transparent structure that lets light enter the eye). Corneal transplants are the most frequently performed transplant surgery, with more than 32,000 performed annually in the United States.

Problems associated with transplantation: The major potential problem is rejection of the transplant. A person's immune system considers an allograft or xenograft a foreign object. It mounts an immune response against it, just as it would if the invader were a virus or bacterium. To limit the problem, a blood test called tissue typing looks at proteins called antigens, which are found on the surfaces of cells. Each human has a pattern of inherited antigens. The greater the similarity between the antigen pattern of a recipient and donor, the weaker the immune response and the less likely that the transplanted tissue will be rejected. The recipient is also given medications called immunosuppressives to counteract the immune response.

Suppressing the immune response to avoid graft rejection, however, creates its own problems. It weakens the body's ability to combat infections. It also increases the risk of cancer. Another problem is graft-versus-host disease. This mimics the body's rejection response. That is, the graft considers the recipient's body tissues as foreign and attacks them. This is a particularly serious problem with bone marrow grafts.

Postsurgical treatment and recovery: After receiving a transplant, the patient focuses on learning how to manage medications and their side effects. A transplant patient faces a lifelong risk of rejecting the implant, though the risk is greatest during the first postoperative year.

Outlook: Improved surgical techniques, a better understanding of the immune system, and more effective antirejection drugs have greatly improved survival rates. But an insufficient supply of donor organs means that many people die while waiting for them. In 2006 in the United States alone, more than 89,000 patients were waiting for a transplant of a vital organ, with nearly 4,000 new patients added to the waiting list each month. An average of 17 people die each day while awaiting a transplant.

Osteoarthritis

(os-tee-oh-ahr-THRIY-tihs)

DISEASE

TYPE: MECHANICAL

See also
Back and spine problems
Bone diseases
Bones
Cartilage
Exercise and health
Prostheses ("replacement body parts")
Skeleton

Where two bones meet at a movable joint, both surfaces are smooth and covered with a layer of cartilage—dense, resilient connective tissue. Although this layer constantly renews itself, at some point in life the process at one or more of the joints starts to fail. Smooth surfaces and close connections gradually degenerate. The result is osteoarthritis ("inflammation of the bone joints"). Affected joints become inflamed, swollen, and painful, and they progressively stiffen.

Cause: Osteoarthritis may be a natural part of the aging process. Joints normally allow bones to move with a minimum of damage to themselves, but eventually fail. The wear and tear of daily use certainly contributes to the disease, but its basic, underlying cause is unknown.

Joints are more likely to be affected if they are under unusual stress. Ballet dancers tend to have osteoarthritis in their feet and ankles; football players, in their shoulders as well as knees and hips. Often, osteoarthritis makes a delayed appearance in joints that have been injured earlier in accidents.

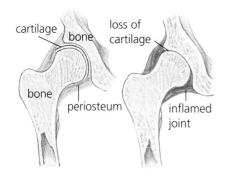

cartilage
bone
loss of cartilage
bone
periosteum
inflamed joint

The wear and tear at the joints that produce osteoarthritis result in the ends of bones becoming closer, causing them to interfere with each other during movement.

Incidence: Osteoarthritis is the most prevalent type of arthritis and one of the most common diseases worldwide. An estimated 66 million Americans—nearly 1 in 3 adults—are affected, many of them undiagnosed. Incidence increases with age. In the United States, all races appear to be equally affected. However, incidence is higher in the Japanese but lower in East Indians, southern Chinese, and South African blacks.

Noticeable symptoms: Osteoarthritis commonly attacks the weight-bearing joints of the knees, hips, and spine. The finger joints are also susceptible, possibly because they are used so much.

The first signs of osteoarthritis are stiffness, swelling, and pain in one or more joints. A person developing the disease may also feel a gritty, grinding sensation in affected joints. Symptoms are generally made worse by work and relieved by rest. The usual pattern is a period of stiffness on rising that subsides as one moves about. But the pain tends to return and get worse as the day goes on, especially if activities put weight or other strain on the joint.

Diagnosis: X-rays may reveal that the bearing surfaces of the bones are rough and pitted rather than smooth. Also evident may be abnormal growths of bone called bone spurs, or *osteophytes* (OS-tee-uh-FIYTS), that form near the joint.

Treatment options: Early stages are usually treated with mild pain relievers such as acetaminophen (Tylenol); aspirin and other nonsteroidal anti-inflammatory drugs (NSAIDS) are less desirable, particularly among elderly patients, because of gastrointestinal side effects. To relieve more severe pain, the cox-2 inhibitor Celebrex may be prescribed. Liniments and ointments may give temporary relief, but the direct application of heat generally gives better results. Massage and moderate exercise are also helpful, as is losing weight if that is called for.

More severe inflammation can sometimes be relieved by injections of corticosteroids into affected joints. But this treatment must be used sparingly, since corticosteroids can themselves hasten the breakdown of cartilage and bone.

Reducing the pressure on inflamed joints often eases the dis-

On the Internet
ARTHRITIS FOUNDATION
www.arthritis.org/conditions/
DiseaseCenter/oa.asp

Did You Know?

Low bone density is not associated with osteoarthritis. Bone density is higher, not lower, in osteoarthritis.

---

comfort. A cane or walking stick can take some of the weight off a sore hip or knee. Many tools and household implements have been adapted so that their handles are more comfortable for stiffened fingers. Even wrapping the handle of a toothbrush or hairbrush with foam rubber can make it more manageable.

When a joint has become seriously deformed by degeneration and bone spurs, the best remedy may be surgery. Sometimes the ends of the bones can be repaired by shaving them smooth and removing bone spurs. For major weight-bearing joints, such as hips or knees, complete replacement often offers longer-lasting relief. The deformed ends of the bones are replaced with artificial parts made of metal or plastic.

Prevention: There is no way to completely prevent osteoarthritis. Regular, moderate exercise can help delay its appearance and slow its later progress. Losing weight—and so reducing pressure on the joints—can also be helpful.

Osteogenesis imperfecta

(OS-tee-uh-JEHN-ih-sihs IHM-puhr-FEHK-tuh)

DISEASE

TYPE: GENETIC

See also
Bones
Genetic diseases
Scoliosis
Skeleton

On the Internet
UNIVERSITY OF MARYLAND
MEDICINE
www.umm.edu/bone/oi.htm

Osteogenesis imperfecta is the collective name for a group of genetic diseases also called *brittle bones.* All have the same basic symptom: The bones break easily and often. A protein called *collagen,* which is essential for bone strength, is produced either in too small a quantity or in an abnormal form.

The effects of osteogenesis imperfecta differ enormously. At one extreme a baby is stillborn or dies in infancy; at the other the susceptibility to fracture is so mild that the underlying problem goes unnoticed.

Cause: Osteogenesis imperfecta results from mutations in one of the two genes responsible for the production of collagen. These genes are dominant; anyone possessing a mutated form will be affected, and any offspring of that person has a 50% chance of inheriting it (see Genetic diseases).

About one in four cases appears spontaneously—with no family history of the defect. Most are likely the result of a new mutation in the mother's egg or the father's sperm. On careful examination, though, some of the victims are found to be the children of very mildly affected parents.

Incidence: It is estimated that 1 in 20,000 persons are born with a mild form of the disease, and 1 in 50,000 babies are born with a severe form that usually results in death in infancy.

Noticeable symptoms: The fragility of the bones may be apparent from infancy on. Those with the more severe types of the defect may show evidence of fractures that have occurred before birth. Defects in the teeth show up when the teeth emerge from the baby's gums.

Collagen is an important part of connective tissue in general. In addition to brittle bones individuals with osteogenesis imperfecta tend to have lax joints, poor muscle tone, and thin, smooth skin, and to suffer from scoliosis, an abnormal curvature of the spine.

Collagen is found in many tissues of the body. It is a component of the whites of the eyes, and osteogenesis imperfecta often causes the whites to be abnormally translucent and bluish in color. Collagen is also essential to the dentin "core" of the teeth, so the teeth of affected individuals tend to be discolored and easily worn down.

For reasons that are not understood, but that may be related to the formation of the bones in the ear, affected individuals often experience progressive hearing loss.

Diagnosis: Biopsies of skin cells may reveal insufficient or abnormal collagen, but the tests are not entirely reliable. DNA analysis may identify the mutation involved; but since the defect can result from many different mutations, it is generally necessary to narrow the search by analyzing samples from several family members, both affected and unaffected.

During pregnancy fetuses with the more severe forms of the defect can sometimes be seen in ultrasound images. The DNA in fetal cells collected by amniocentesis can be analyzed as well.

Treatment options: There is no cure, but often the symptoms can be alleviated. Fractures usually become less of a problem after puberty. Exercises and physical therapy can help build muscle strength and maintain mobility. Lightweight casts and splints are used to support fractures. Hearing loss can be alleviated with hearing aids and sometimes relieved by surgery. Crowns can be placed over weakened teeth. The long limb bones can sometimes be stabilized by inserting metal rods into them.

Osteomalacia

(os-tee-oh-muh-LAY-shuh)

When adults suffer a softening of the bones for any reason, the condition is called osteomalacia. This may occur because of a loss of calcium or, less frequently, a loss of the mineral phosphorus. Children with this condition are said to have rickets, and sometimes osteomalacia is identified as *adult rickets*. Bones of the spine, pelvis, legs, and feet are most often affected, but any bone in the body can become soft.

Cause: Osteomalacia is most often a symptom of lack of vitamin D. Calcium is important for nerve and muscle function and is stored in the bones. But without vitamin D the body cannot utilize the calcium in food. The body compensates for the resulting calcium shortage by taking it from bones. If this situation continues for an extended period, the bones soften from lack of calcium.

Any intestinal disorder that blocks absorption of minerals can lead to osteomalacia. For example, the elderly may have increased risk if they are lactose intolerant and do not get out in the sun very often. Inadequate absorption of fats also can cause osteomalacia because vitamin D is stored in fats. In addition, a kidney problem that raises the acid level of bodily fluids may cause the symptom—the acids eat away the calcium in the bones, softening them. Certain medications may also lead to osteomalacia.

Noticeable symptoms: Tenderness and pain of the affected bones are early symptoms. The patient may also experience a general feeling of weakness.

Because bone growth has been completed in adults, deformities such as those seen in children with rickets are rare. Instead, the softening bones become painful and tend to fracture easily.

Treatment: Osteomalacia caused by a dietary deficiency is easily treated with high doses of vitamin D and calcium supplements. If kidney problems, intestinal problems, or other underlying conditions have caused the bones to soften, a doctor must treat these disorders while also restoring normal levels of vitamin D and calcium.

Prevention: Drinking vitamin D-fortified milk can prevent osteomalacia caused by lack of the vitamin. Getting outside in the sunlight also helps because the skin actually manufactures vitamin D when exposed to sunlight. Sometimes vitamin or mineral supplements are needed.

Osteomyelitis

(os-tee-oh-MIY-uh-LIY-tihs)

Known since ancient times, osteomyelitis is a potentially serious bacterial infection of one or more bones. The infection may involve all or only part of a bone, and various bones can be affected, including the vertebras of the spinal column. Long bones of the legs and arms are the ones most often infected in children; the spine, hip, and foot in adults.

Cause: Bacteria from infections elsewhere in the body sometimes travel through the bloodstream and indirectly start a secondary infection in a bone. For example, a throat infection—especially if caused by staphylococcus or streptococcus bacteria—can sometimes cause osteomyelitis. The same is true of skin infections and other common bacterial diseases. Bacteria may also reach bone through an open wound that exposes bone or that shatters bone (for example, a bullet wound), as a result of a bone fracture that has broken the skin, or by way of an injection when the needle touches bone.

Incidence: The number of people with osteomyelitis is uncertain, with estimates in the United States ranging from 20,000 to 50,000. Incidence is believed to be similar in other developed countries but higher in places where proper wound care is inadequate. Incidence after foot puncture may be as high as 16%—and up to 40% in people with diabetes. Children and adolescents are more likely to suffer osteomyelitis than adults.

Noticeable symptoms: Onset of symptoms tends to be more sudden in children and may include severe pain and swelling in the affected bone, fever, and chills. Fever is absent in up to a third of cases. In adults the disease may begin as nothing more than a vague, localized pain in a bone.

Diagnosis: Blood tests that reveal certain bacteria in the system will help a doctor confirm a diagnosis of osteomyelitis. Signs of bone infection show up on x-rays about ten days to two weeks after symptoms first appear. The physician may also need to surgically remove and examine a sample of infected bone or tissue from an abscess associated with the infected bone.

Treatment options: Antibiotics are usually successful in treating osteomyelitis. Patients may have to take the antibiotics for three or more weeks. Sometimes abscesses must be drained surgically. If sections of dead bone slow healing, they may have to be surgically removed. Damaged sections of bone sometimes grow back if blood vessels to the area are intact.

Prevention: Prompt treatment of "staph," "strep," and other infections can help prevent these bacteria from migrating to a bone and causing osteomyelitis.

Osteoporosis

(os-tee-oh-puh-ROH-sihs)

DISEASE

TYPE: GENETIC; MECHANICAL

See also
Back and spine problems
Bones
Diet and health
Exercise and health
Hormonal system
Ovaries
Skeleton
Tobacco and disease
Vitamin-deficiency diseases

On the Internet
OSTEOPOROSIS CANADA
www.osteoporosis.ca/english/
About%20Osteoporosis/FAQs/
default.asp?s=1

In osteoporosis, bones become progressively thinner and less dense. A related condition, *osteopenia* (os-tee-oh-PEE-nee-uh), is low bone mass without progressive loss.

Cause: Bone is not the stable substance that it appears to be—the body continually makes new bone and removes parts of existing bone to use elsewhere. Osteoporosis occurs when more of the minerals calcium and phosphate in bone are lost than replaced, causing bones to become thin. Unlike osteomalacia, soft bones that bend under stress, osteoporosis is a reduction in bone mass.

Osteoporosis is caused by a combination of genetic and environmental factors. It appears to be a result of the aging process in some people, especially women. During menopause—a life stage that generally begins in the late forties—women begin to produce less of the female hormone estrogen. Research shows that this alters the balance between new bone formation and use of material from bone elsewhere in the body.

Hormone diseases that result in excess adrenal, thyroid, or parathyroid hormones can produce osteoporosis as well.

Risk factors: Women who are underweight, physically inactive, or have a family history of the disease are at greater risk. Women who smoke or drink beverages with alcohol or caffeine increase their chances of bone loss as well. This is because nicotine, alcohol, and caffeine interfere with natural absorption of calcium. Women of European ancestry have a greater predisposition for the disease than women of other genetic backgrounds. So do women who enter menopause early.

Incidence: Osteoporosis is most common among older people, especially women, who start with 30% less bone mass than men and lose it faster after menopause. Caucasian and Asian women

Don't smoke

Avoid alcohol

No caffeine

Did You Know?

A hunched back is a form of the condition called kyphosis. Osteoporosis isn't the only cause of a rounded back. Postural kyphosis develops when poor posture or slouching causes abnormal formation of the vertebrae.

have less bone mass than African American women and thus are at greater risk. An estimated 10 million Americans—8 million women and 2 million men—have osteoporosis. Almost 34 million more are believed to have osteopenia, placing them at increased risk for osteoporosis. About 1.3 million fractures due to osteoporosis occur each year in the United States.

Noticeable symptoms: Early osteoporosis shows no obvious symptoms. As the disease progresses, there may be back pain, loss of height, stooped posture, or noticeable curvature of the spine. Some women appear to have a hump made of the bones of the spine, sometimes referred to as "dowager's hump." Each of these symptoms occurs because the vertebras, the small bones that make up the spine, have lost bone mass to the point where they have begun to collapse on one another. Another symptom is bone fracture in the wrist or hip caused by a light fall.

Diagnosis: Women should have measurements made of their bone mineral density after menopause if they have had a fracture or at age 65 even when there are no other signs of osteoporosis. This entails taking a special kind of x-ray that shows the amount of calcium in the skeleton. Ordinary x-rays can reveal fractures that are not otherwise recognized, such as collapsing vertebras.

Treatment options: A basic treatment is to take supplements to replace some of the hard minerals lost from the bones. Calcium in the form of calcium carbonate or calcium citrate is available as over-the-counter tablets. This may be combined with vitamin therapy, especially vitamin D, which helps the body use calcium. Another kind of treatment is estrogen replacement therapy. This treatment gives the body more of the hormones that are lost when a woman goes through menopause. It is most effective if begun at menopause since most bone loss occurs in the first half dozen years after menopause. This therapy is not always recommended because of various risk factors, including cancer.

Certain medicines have been shown to halt or reduce osteoporosis in older women, including alendronate (trade name: Fosamax) and raloxifene (trade name: Evista). Raloxifene acts by binding to estrogen receptors and has been shown to reduce fractures of the vertebras by almost 50%. It has many of the benefits of estrogen replacement therapy with fewer possible side effects.

Exercise

Prevention: Weight-bearing exercises are recommended for the prevention of osteoporosis. These include walking, jogging, aerobics, rope jumping, or weight lifting several times a week for about half an hour. Before anyone over 40 takes on a new regimen of exercise, however, a doctor should be consulted.

A healthy diet combined with exercise, if started early in life, may prevent osteoporosis, but in any case a good diet with plenty of minerals from dark green leafy vegetables, dairy products, and salmon or sardines is one part of any effort to keep the disease at bay.

When people do show signs of osteoporosis, they can reduce the risk of injury or falls by taking some important precautions. Keeping a house well lighted and floors clear of obstacles, and avoiding slick or icy pathways, can prevent falls that could cause bone fracture. Women should wear low-heeled shoes, and both men and women should make sure that any vision problems have been corrected.

Otitis externa (swimmer's ear)

(oh-TIY-tihs ihk-STUR-nuh)

DISEASE

TYPE: INFECTION (BACTERIAL; FUNGAL; VIRAL)

See also
Deafness
Earache
E. coli infection
Edema
Fungus diseases
Otitis media
"Staph"

Acute otitis externa is an inflammation of the outer ear. It is most prevalent during swimming season, when people frequent pools, lakes, and the ocean. It is commonly known as swimmer's ear.

Cause: The delicate skin in the ear canal—the tube leading from the outside toward the eardrum—normally is covered with a protective waxy secretion called earwax, or *cerumen* (suh-ROO-muhn). When the ear canal is repeatedly exposed to water, the earwax is washed away. The skin is exposed and becomes a breeding ground for germs. Using cotton swabs to clean the ear canal or putting items into the ear that can scratch the canal also increase the risk of otitis externa.

Otitis externa usually is caused by a bacterium such as *Escherichia coli* (*E. coli*), *Staphylococcus aureus*, or *Pseudomonas aeruginosa*. In some cases the causative agent is a fungus such as members of the genera *Candida* and *Aspergillus*. Two kinds of viruses, herpes virus and varicella zoster, also cause otitis externa, and it may be one symptom of a chronic skin disease, such as eczema.

Noticeable symptoms: Typically, the outer ear becomes red, swollen, and itchy. The ear canal becomes clogged with yellow,

On the Internet
AMERICAN ACADEMY
OF FAMILY PHYSICIANS
familydoctor.org/657.xml

foul-smelling debris. The debris may prevent sound from moving through the ear canal, resulting in partial loss of hearing. There may also be pain in the outer ear, tenderness and swelling of nearby lymph nodes, and headache on the side of the affected ear.

Treatment options: Otitis externa usually is treated by thoroughly cleaning the ear and then applying eardrops, which, for bacterial infections, consist of antibiotics combined with corticosteroids. Symptoms clear up, and the patient is cured in three to five days. If pain is severe, an analgesic may also be prescribed.

Prevention: Proper care of the ears will help prevent otitis externa. It is recommended that people with a history of the disease use over-the-counter eardrops containing a mixture of alcohol and glycerin after bathing or swimming.

Otitis media

(oh-TIY-tihs MEE-dee-uh)

DISEASE

TYPE: INFECTIOUS (VIRAL;
BACTERIAL; FUNGAL)

See also
Allergies
Bacteria and disease
Common cold
Congestion
Earache
Fungus diseases
Hay fever
Hemophilus influenzae **type B**
Infants and disease
Influenza
Labyrinthitis
Reye's syndrome
"Strep"
Viruses and disease
"Virus" infection

When a child complains of an earache, many times otitis media is the cause. Otitis media is inflammation of the middle ear. The middle ear is the part of the ear just beyond the eardrum that amplifies and transfers sound vibrations from the eardrum to the inner ear, where the vibrations are changed into nerve impulses.

Cause: In children the eustachian (yoo-STAY-shuhn) tube, which connects the back of the throat with the ear, is very short and nearly horizontal. Along this short pathway microorganisms from the throat easily travel to the ear. Acute otitis media is usually caused by bacteria or viruses that have invaded the middle ear. Chronic or recurring otitis media may be caused by viruses, funguses, or allergies.

Incidence: Otitis media is a common disease of children, occurring most frequently in the first four years of life, before the immune system is fully developed. It occurs mostly in winter and early spring. Children with enlarged adenoids (lymph glands near the nose) are more likely to develop otitis media.

Noticeable symptoms: A young child may tug at the ear, become irritable, cry repeatedly, experience diarrhea or vomiting, and run a fever. Older children may express feelings of pain or of fullness in the ear. If the disease has progressed, especially if both ears are involved, sounds are heard as muffled, and dizziness may occur.

Diagnosis: A physician can examine the ears with an otoscope to detect redness and swelling of the eardrum caused by otitis media. If the eardrum is punctured, there is also a discharge of pus from the ear. If there is reason to suspect hearing loss, tests of that function may also be administered.

Treatment options: To relieve symptoms, over-the-counter eardrops and nonaspirin fever and pain reducers may help combat pain. ***Do not give aspirin to a child with fever.*** A decongestant may help relieve pain as well.

Any person showing signs of otitis media should be seen by a physician and treated promptly. For bacterial infections antibiotics are usually prescribed. If an infection does not clear up within ten days (the usual course of antibiotics), a different antibiotic may be prescribed. Often the eardrum is slit or a small tube is inserted in the eardrum to relieve fluid pressure. The tube will fall out by itself or be removed when fluid has drained; it causes no scarring or damage to the eardrum.

Stages and progress: Otitis media usually occurs in a child during the first few days of a viral upper respiratory infection such as a cold or "flu." While the immune system fights the virus, bacteria take advantage. The infection travels to the eardrum and mastoids, cavities near the ear, and may produce a yellow-green discharge from the ear. As the disease progresses, there may be painful swelling and a tumorlike cyst inside the middle ear. If the infection is chronic, scarring or breaking of the eardrum can lead to deafness. Some kinds of bacteria may also spread the infection to other parts of the body.

The most serious health problems occur if the infection spreads to the mastoids or other parts of the body. ***Call a doctor if the bone behind the ear (mastoid process) is sore or if a sick child reports dizziness or sudden blurring of vision.***

There is also a learning and psychological cost to the partial deafness that may accompany otitis media.

Prevention: Breast-feeding reduces the risk of ear infections in young children, as do hand washing and other steps designed to decrease transmission of cold viruses and other germs. In 2006 it was reported that an experimental vaccine against *Streptococcus pneumoniae* and *Hemophilus influenzae* provided infants with significant protection against acute otitis media.

Avoid aspirin

On the Internet
NATIONAL INSTITUTE
ON DEAFNESS AND OTHER
COMMUNICATION DISORDERS
www.nidcd.nih.gov/health/
hearing/otitismedia.asp

Phone doctor

Otosclerosis

(OH-toh-skluh-ROH-sihs)

DISEASE

TYPE: GENETIC

See also
Deafness
Tinnitus

On the Internet
NATIONAL INSTITUTE ON DEAFNESS AND OTHER COMMUNICATION DISORDERS
www.nidcd.nih.gov/health/hearing/otosclerosis.asp

Otosclerosis is a common cause of hearing loss in teens and young adults. It occurs when the stirrup—one of the tiny bones in the middle ear—becomes unable to transmit sound waves.

Cause: Spongy bone tissue grows around the stirrup, preventing it from vibrating and thus passing on sound waves. As the bony growth gets larger there is progressive hearing loss. The problem may affect one or both ears of a person. Otosclerosis is generally believed to be a hereditary condition, although it is not unusual to see the disease in only one member of a family.

Incidence: About 10% of Caucasians have otosclerosis but only 1% develop significant hearing loss as a result of the disease. Incidence is less in other ethnic groups; for example, incidence in blacks is only 1% that of Caucasians. In all groups, if one ear is affected, the other ear is affected 80 to 90% of the time. Symptoms become apparent between ages 15 and 45, usually starting around age 20. Women are affected twice as often as men, with hearing often worsening rapidly during pregnancy.

Noticeable symptoms: Hearing loss is the most common symptom. After the disease has progressed, there may be abnormal or loud speech. Hearing noises in the ear, such as ringing (tinnitus), is also a late symptom.

Diagnosis: A doctor will also perform a series of hearing tests to determine if the hearing loss is due to a mechanical problem or a problem in the transmission of sound to the brain.

Treatment options: An operation called a *stapedectomy* (STAY-pih-DEHK-tuh-mee) usually cures otosclerosis—another name for the stirrup bone is *stapes* (STAY-peez). This operation is performed under local anesthesia and usually does not require an overnight hospital stay. A surgeon removes the abnormal stirrup bone and replaces it with an artificial one. Between 90 and 95% of people with the surgery regain close to normal hearing within two to four weeks after the operation. The delay in experiencing the results is due to swelling in the middle ear, which takes time to disappear. It is best to do one ear at a time since sometimes the operation fails and removes all hearing in that ear.

Ovarian cysts

(oh-VAIR-ee-uhn SIHSTS)

DISEASE

TYPE: UNKNOWN

See also
Cysts
Ovaries
Peritonitis
Swellings
Tumor, benign

On the Internet
NATIONAL WOMEN'S HEALTH
INFORMATION CENTER
www.4woman.gov/faq/
ovarian_cysts.htm

A cyst is a sac that is filled with a fluid, which may be very thick. When a cyst is found in or on a woman's ovary, it is called an ovarian cyst. Despite the name, some ovarian cysts are solid.

Cause: The cause of ovarian cysts is unknown. The most common type, called *functional cysts,* occur when ordinary menstrual changes in parts of the ovary continue instead of stopping.

Incidence: Although an ovarian cyst can occur at any age, it is most common in females 20 to 35 years of age.

Noticeable symptoms: Frequently, there are no symptoms. Sometimes there is pain and swelling in the lower abdomen. If the cyst is large, it may press on the bladder, causing a sensation of having to urinate. Or the cyst could cause urinary retention, depending on its size and location. Irregular menstruation and other symptoms of a decrease in hormone production could occur. A cyst that becomes twisted could cause severe pain, nausea, and fever.

Diagnosis: When a doctor performs an examination, he or she may feel a lump on the ovary or an enlargement of the ovary. The next step is usually an ultrasound scan. Sound waves bounced off the ovary provide a picture of the ovary and the cyst if there is one. To view the ovary in greater detail, a *laparoscopy* may be performed. In this procedure the physician views the inside of the abdomen through a tiny camera.

Treatment options: Frequently, if the cyst is within the ovary, there are only mild symptoms or none. This type of cyst usually disappears on its own in a few months. Cysts that cause pain or continue to grow are surgically removed.

The removal of an ovarian cyst is performed through a small incision in a type of operation called a *laparotomy* (LAAP-uh-ROT-uh-mee). This is done if the cyst is causing pain or other symptoms. In some cases a physician might recommend that the entire ovary and fallopian tube be removed so that the cyst does not recur. If this surgery is performed, pregnancy can still occur because the other ovary still exists.

Stages and progress: If an ovarian cyst becomes large, there is the potential for bursting. This causes fluid to enter the abdomen, putting the woman at risk for the infection peritonitis. Twisting of the cyst may also occur, making symptoms more severe.

Even though ovarian cysts are common and do not always require medical intervention, they need to be evaluated by a doctor. There are other diseases that share the same signs and symptoms that will need to be ruled out. Also, some cysts are potentially cancerous and thus should be evaluated and treated promptly.

Prevention: The hormone combinations in oral contraceptives can often prevent (or even shrink) functional cysts.

Ovaries

(OH-vuh-reez)

BODY SYSTEM

The two ovaries are the main glands that produce sex hormones in women, corresponding to the testes in men—the general name that covers both sets of glands is gonads (GOH-naadz). The ovaries are the repository of hundreds of thousands of precursors to egg cells, called ova (OH-vuh; singular: ovum). Each month (28 days, usually), from the time a girl reaches puberty (around age 10 to 13), one of the ovaries produces and releases a single ovum. After this has happened some 400 or so times, a woman's ovaries shut down. This time in a woman's life is known as menopause.

Size and location: Each ovary is about the size of an almond or somewhat larger. The ovaries are located symmetrically in the pelvis at either side of and somewhat above the uterus, which is itself at the end of the birth canal and just above the bladder. Each ovary is at one end of a fallopian tube, which has the uterus at its other end—although the tube passes around the ovary, embracing it to some degree.

Role: About once every four weeks in a woman of reproductive age the pituitary gland, located just below the brain, releases a hormone called *follicle-stimulating hormone* (FSH) into the blood. When FSH reaches the ovary, it stimulates several of the *primitive Graafian follicles* to begin the development, called ripening, of their contents; these are the precursors of ova. Each precursor egg is in its own follicle. After about ten days one ovum ripens, and the others fade away.

When the ovum is ripe, it breaks out of the follicle. The follicle soon fills with a special yellow material called the *corpus luteum* (KAWR-puhs LOO-tee-uhm, Latin for "yellowish body"). The corpus luteum makes a hormone that signals the uterus that an egg is on the way.

From time to time more than one egg ripens during the same month, creating the possibility of *fraternal twins* or other multiple births. *Identical twins* result from a different mechanism—a fertilized egg splits into two parts that continue development.

Conditions that affect the ovaries: The ovaries, like the testes, are subject to cysts (fluid-filled sacs), which are common, and cancer, which is rare, but often deadly. Ovarian cancer is not easy to detect in early stages, when removal of the cancerous ovary and nearby reproductive organs and lymph nodes might produce a cure. Undetected ovarian cancer may signal itself with pain and considerable swelling of the lower abdomen. ***See a physician if these symptoms develop.***

PID (pelvic inflammatory disease) is any infection of the uterus, where such infections usually begin, fallopian tubes, and ovaries. It is fairly common, especially among the young and sexually active. Since it can damage the ovaries or fallopian tubes, PID also requires treatment as soon as symptoms develop.

Phone doctor

Pain

SYMPTOM

The International Association for the Study of Pain offers the following definition of pain: "An unpleasant sensory and emotional experience associated with actual or potential tissue damage or described in terms of such damage." But no simple definition can do justice to the enormous variety and complexity of pain, which is a major feature of many diseases and other disorders and, when it becomes persistent and intractable, may be considered a disease in itself.

Acute and chronic pain: Pain is classified as either *acute* or *chronic*. Acute pain comes on relatively quickly, is provoked by a specific stimulus such as infection or injury, and eventually

On the Internet

MEDLINE PLUS

www.nlm.nih.gov/medlineplus/
pain.html

subsides once the stimulus is removed or healing takes place. Acute pain is part of the body's necessary defenses. It warns of the need to escape from dangers such as fire or sharp objects, it tells that we are sick or injured, and it impels us to seek rest and relief until we recover.

Chronic pain, by contrast, persists without any identifiably positive function. It may start as an acute condition that does not subside or heal, but that continues or even gets worse, as in shingles, which sometimes develops into postherpetic (POHST-huhr-PEHT-ihk) neuralgia. Chronic pain may involve an inborn predisposition triggered by a variety of factors into repeated attacks, as in migraine headaches. It may be caused by some ongoing illness, such as rheumatoid arthritis, osteoarthritis, displacement of a spinal disk, or cancer. It may be an aftereffect of damage to the nervous system, such as various forms of neuralgia. And sometimes it is *idiopathic* (IHD-ee-uh-PAATH-ihk)—it occurs without any clear cause and appears to be a disease in itself.

How pain is sensed: The sensation of pain usually begins at the ends of specialized nerve cells, called *peripheral neurons,* that are sensitive to irritating stimuli of varying kinds, ranging from inflammation to excessive heat or pressure. When the ends of these peripheral neurons are stimulated, they transmit a signal to the spinal cord, which passes the message along to the brain. Most pain impulses pass through a part of the brain called the thalamus; they then are processed in other parts, including the cerebral cortex.

The experience of pain is not a simple transmission of impulses from peripheral nerves to the spinal cord and brain, however. Along the way, particularly at the synapses between the pain-sensing neurons, neurotransmitters produced by other neurons may either intensify or temper the pain signals. Many treatments for pain either encourage the natural production of pain-tempering neurotransmitters or mimic their action.

Some pain impulses provoke a reaction without reaching the brain. When one flinches away from contact with a sharp or hot object, the stimulus to the spinal cord triggers a response in motor nerves going back to the affected area. This immediate, unconscious response is called a *reflex arc,* and it is another part of the body's natural defenses.

The treatment of pain: Many therapies are used to relieve pain, and they are often combined for greater effectiveness. Numerous medical centers now have pain clinics where teams of specialists offer coordinated treatment to patients suffering from chronic pain.

Anti-inflammatory drugs: Inflammation represents a natural response by the body's immune system against infection and injury. Its characteristic symptoms are swelling, redness, and pain. The pain results mainly from irritating hormones called *prostaglandins* (PROS-tuh-GLAAN-dihns). Anti-inflammatory drugs inhibit their production. There are two main types of such drugs. One is composed of corticosteroids, such as prednisone and cortisone; these are extremely powerful but can have serious adverse side effects. More commonly used for pain relief are the nonsteroidal anti-inflammatory drugs (NSAIDs). The best known of these is aspirin, but they also include other over-the-counter drugs such as ibuprofen and prescription drugs such as indomethacin.

Acetaminophen: Best known by the trade name Tylenol, acetaminophen reduces the perception of pain in the central nervous system, particularly the brain.

Opioids: The term opioid means "opiumlike," and the most familiar opioids are opium itself and its derivatives, codeine and morphine. Opioids block the transmission of pain signals in the central nervous system. They are extremely effective against severe pain, such as the pain of advanced cancer. When used to relieve such pain, they pose little if any danger of dependence, much less addiction.

Antidepressants: Drugs that are primarily used to treat mental depression have also been found helpful in relieving pain, probably because of their effects on certain neurotransmitters in the brain. Among the more widely used are tricyclic antidepressants such as amitriptyline (trade name: Elavil).

Anticonvulsants: The drugs used to treat epilepsy are sometimes used to relieve the intense, chronic pain of some forms of neuralgia that result from damage to peripheral sensory nerves.

Capsaicin: The substance that makes hot peppers hot is blended into topical creams for the relief of arthritis. It may work as a counterirritant—a relatively mild irritant that leads to the release of neurotransmitters that temper the transmission of more severe pain signals.

Local anesthetics: Numbing anesthetics, such as lidocaine, injected into painful areas or at major relay points for pain impulses provide at least temporary relief. They are used most often to alleviate acute pain, but they can also be helpful against chronic pain such as arthritis.

Physical therapy: The techniques of physical therapy, including applications of heat and cold, massage, joint manipulation, supervised exercise, and posture correction are widely used to relieve both acute and chronic pain of the muscles and joints. Massage, for example, is believed to stimulate sensory nerves that respond to touch and pressure, causing them to produce neurotransmitters that reduce the intensity of pain sensations.

Acupuncture: This traditional therapy is undeniably effective in relieving pain in some patients.

Electrical stimulation: For reasons that are not well understood, passing mild electrical impulses through parts of the body can produce pain relief. The most widely used and least invasive technique is transcutaneous electrical nerve stimulation (TENS), in which pulses of electricity pass between electrodes attached to the skin. But for severe chronic pain, spinal cord or deep brain stimulation, using implanted electrodes, may be employed.

Psychological support: The experience of pain is mental as well as physical, and its treatment often includes techniques to reduce its psychological impact. Many of these techniques are intended to improve the ability to reduce and cope with stress. They include relaxation training, distraction through guided imagery or hypnosis, and biofeedback.

Nerve blocks: When severe and enduring pain cannot be relieved in any other way, the pathways of pain-sensing nerves may be permanently blocked by injected chemicals or by surgery, usually at or near the junctions between the peripheral nerves of the body and the central nerves of the spinal cord.

Palpitations
(paal-pih-TAY-shuhnz)

SYMPTOM

When your heart feels as if it is pounding rapidly or beating very slowly or irregularly, you are having palpitations—also known as skips, flips, or flutters. Palpitations occur when the electrical signals in the heart do not work as they should and the normal rhythm of the heartbeat is disturbed.

Call ambulance

No stress

No caffeine

Don't smoke

Phone doctor

Parts affected: Palpitations are usually felt in the chest. As the rhythm of the heartbeat is disturbed, it affects the way in which the heart pumps blood through the blood vessels. Just as you can feel your heartbeat as your *pulse* at points on the body where an artery is near the surface, so you may feel palpitations at the wrist, on the side of the neck, or at other pulse points.

Related symptoms: Palpitations are very common and are often harmless, lasting only a few seconds or minutes, with no other symptoms. Shortness of breath is common, as are dizziness or fainting episodes when there is a sequence of many palpitations. Fluttering may produce a tickling sensation near the heart.

Associations: Being nervous or excited can cause rapid heartbeats. If you get palpitations and are also losing weight, you may have goiter or an overactive thyroid gland. A fever due to an infection or illness can cause palpitations.

Frequent occurrences of palpitations, especially when accompanied by other symptoms, may indicate a heart disorder that needs treatment. In one type of disorder the heartbeat begins in the ventricles instead of in the atria. This produces a beat that has no regular rhythm but jumps about in a disorganized way. ***This condition needs the immediate attention of a physician or emergency heathcare worker.***

Prevention and possible actions: Avoid situations that cause undue anxiety if possible. The caffeine in coffee, tea, and cola drinks and the nicotine in tobacco can temporarily affect the heart's rhythm. Avoid them entirely or use them in moderation.

Certain drugs such as cocaine and amphetamines can produce dangerous palpitations and should be avoided. If palpitations occur frequently, or if they last more than a few minutes, consult your physician. You may need medication or other treatment.

Relief of symptoms: During an attack try lying down and relaxing. Some people find that holding their breath or bathing their face in cold water stops the palpitations. Beta blockers are often prescribed if palpitations recur frequently.

Pancreas

(PAANG-kree-uhs)

On the Internet
NATIONAL PANCREAS
FOUNDATION
www.pancreasfoundation.org/
learn/pancreas.shtml

The pancreas has a dual role—it helps digest food and also secretes hormones that, among other things, affect the level of sugar in the blood. Pancreatic juice, which helps digest food, is secreted into the small intestine by way of the tube called the *pancreatic duct*. But the pancreas also has about a million tiny groups of specialized cells, called *islets of Langerhans* (LAHNG-uhr-HAHNS), that are scattered throughout the organ. These cells secrete their three hormones directly into the bloodstream.

Size and location: The pancreas is 5 to 7 inches long and 1.5 inches wide. It is in the abdomen, behind the stomach and near the spleen and duodenum (upper section of the small intestine).

Role: Digestive juices secreted by the pancreas combine with enzymes from the small intestine to complete the job of breaking down proteins, carbohydrates, and fats. Substances in pancreatic juice also help neutralize stomach acids that pass from the stomach into the small intestine.

The islets of Langerhans produce three hormones. *Glucagon* (GLOO-kuh-GON) raises the level of glucose (sugar) in the blood. *Insulin* stimulates muscle and other cells to utilize glucose from the blood. *Somatostatin* (soh-MAAT-uh-STAAT-n) helps regulate the secretion of glucagon and insulin.

Conditions that affect the pancreas: Alcoholism, gallstones, and viral infections can cause a serious inflammation of the pancreas called pancreatitis. When gallstones block the bile duct, which the pancreatic duct empties into, the flow of pancreatic juices is stopped; this may also lead to pancreatitis.

Diabetes mellitus is a serious common disorder that occurs when the islets of Langerhans fail to produce enough insulin. Hypoglycemia, or too little sugar in the blood, can result from an overproduction of insulin. Tumors on the islets themselves, or large tumors on other organs near the pancreas, can induce release of excess insulin.

Cancer of the pancreas is seldom detected in its early stages and prognosis following diagnosis is poor. Heavy alcohol use, smoking, and high levels of dietary fat appear to be risk factors.

Pancreatitis

(PAANG-kree-uh-TIY-tihs)

DISEASE

TYPE: COMBINATION

See also
Alcoholism
Digestive system
Gallstones
Jaundice
Mumps
Pancreas

Phone doctor

On the Internet
NATIONAL PANCREAS
FOUNDATION
www.pancreasfoundation.org/
learn/pancreas.shtml

An inflammation of the pancreas called pancreatitis can produce severe abdominal pain. Depending on the cause, the attack may be brief or a recurring problem.

Cause: Pancreatitis occurs when the potent digestive enzymes in the pancreas begin to attack the gland itself. Acute pancreatitis, in which the pancreas often returns to normal following treatment, is usually caused by gallstones, alcohol abuse, certain medications, or occasionally mumps.

In chronic pancreatitis, the pancreas becomes permanently damaged and unable to supply a sufficient amount of hormones and digestive juices. The main cause of chronic pancreatitis is alcoholism; other causes include trauma or cystlike structures that block the pancreatic duct, and inherited factors.

Incidence: About 80,000 Americans suffer acute pancreatitis annually. Chronic pancreatitis affects about 8 out of every 100,000 persons, or about 24,000 Americans.

Noticeable symptoms: Severe abdominal pain that develops suddenly is the usual sign of pancreatitis. Any movement—even coughing or breathing deeply—may intensify the pain. Nausea, vomiting, fever, sweating, and rapid pulse also are common. Abdominal swelling and jaundice may occur. *It is important to seek medical help as soon as possible.* Acute pancreatitis is sometimes fatal.

Chronic pancreatitis is indicated by frequent pain in the back or abdomen coupled with weight loss caused by poor digestion.

Diagnosis: If a physician suspects pancreatitis, you will be admitted to a hospital. Tests will be conducted to confirm the diagnosis and to determine the underlying cause of the illness.

Treatment options: You will probably be given painkillers plus medications to reduce the production of pancreatic juices. Shock will be treated with intravenous fluids. Several weeks may pass before all symptoms of an attack subside. During this time you will not be allowed to eat. Instead, your nutritional needs will be supplied intravenously. After hospitalization you should not drink alcohol or eat large meals for several days.

Avoid alcohol

For chronic pancreatitis the doctor may prescribe enzyme tablets to help digest food plus painkillers to combat pain. A special diet that restricts the intake of fat and protein will be recommended. You will be told to avoid alcohol. Part of the pancreas may need to be removed.

Panic attacks

DISEASE

TYPE: MENTAL

See also
Brain
Delusions
Mental illnesses
Obsessive-compulsive disorder
PMS (premenstrual syndrome)

On the Internet
MAYO CLINIC
www.mayoclinic.com/health/
panic-attacks/DS00338

People who suffer panic attacks, a serious emotional disorder, feel fear and anxiety that can lead to trembling, sweating, palpitations, and shortness of breath when they undergo an episode. If there were real evidence of danger, such emotional and physical reactions would be appropriate, a result of the "fight-or-flight response." But people suffering panic attacks have these extreme reactions when there is little or nothing to fear.

Cause: Recurrent panic attacks apparently result from defects in brain chemistry. The exact cause is unknown but the disease runs in families, indicating a genetic component. There may also be an unusual hormonal response. A deep-seated emotional problem or other conflict may also contribute to the onset of attacks.

Incidence: Worldwide, an estimated 1 out of every 75 people experience a panic attack at some time in their lives, though most never develop repeated attacks. In the United States, about 2% of the population is affected by panic disorder each year. Women are twice as likely as men to suffer from the disease.

Noticeable symptoms: During a panic attack, a person may experience a racing heartbeat, heart palpitations, difficulty in breathing, tingling in the hands or feet, nausea, trembling, sweating, or sudden chills. He or she may feel anxiety, fear, or paralyzing terror. An attack usually lasts about 5 to 20 minutes, but may continue for up to an hour.

Associations: Panic attacks may occur with an accompanying fear of open places (agoraphobia) or along with depression. Some medical conditions can trigger episodes, as can drug withdrawal. In about 25% of cases patients also suffer obsessive-compulsive disorder.

Treatment options: Various antidepressants, which alter brain biochemistry, have proven effective in treating panic attacks. When combined with behavior therapy, in which the patient learns relaxation techniques and to confront his or her fears, there is often long-lasting relief. Psychotherapy may help resolve any underlying emotional conflicts.

Paralysis

SYMPTOM

See also
ALS (amyotrophic lateral sclerosis)
Bell's palsy
Botulism
Cancers
Cerebral palsy
Guillain-Barré syndrome
Narcolepsy
Neuropathy
Parkinson's disease
Poliomyelitis ("polio")
Sciatica
Spinal cord
Stem cells
Stroke
TIA (transient ischemic attack)
Tumor, benign

On the Internet
MEDLINE PLUS
www.nlm.nih.gov/medlineplus/
paralysis.html

Paralysis is the partial or complete loss of muscle function in a limb or some other part of the body. It is the result of damage to parts of the central nervous system caused by various infectious diseases, tumors, or severe accidents, such as a fall from a horse that results in a broken neck.

Cause: There are two main categories of paralysis:

■ *Central paralysis* results from damage to the brain or spinal column and usually involves paralysis of an entire limb instead of just individual muscles. Types of central paralysis include *paraplegia* (PAAR-uh-PLEE-jee-uh), paralysis of both legs; *quadriplegia,* paralysis of all four limbs; and *hemiplegia,* paralysis of one entire side of the body.

■ *Peripheral paralysis* occurs when a nerve or nerves leading to specific parts of the body are damaged in an accident, by disease, or even by exposure to certain chemicals. Localized paralysis, called *ischemic* (ih-SKEE-mihk) *paralysis,* occurs when blood flow to a particular area is stopped.

Severe emotional problems may also produce paralysis. With *hysterical paralysis* there is no physical damage to the nervous system. With successful psychotherapy the patient should regain full use of the affected part.

Parts affected: Paralysis can affect any part of the body, one whole side, or, as in the case of quadriplegia, nearly the whole body. Control of muscles and sensations in the affected area are often lost. Depending on the cause, the paralysis can be temporary or permanent.

The underlying cause may affect the brain, the spinal column, or the nerves that deliver directions to the muscles.

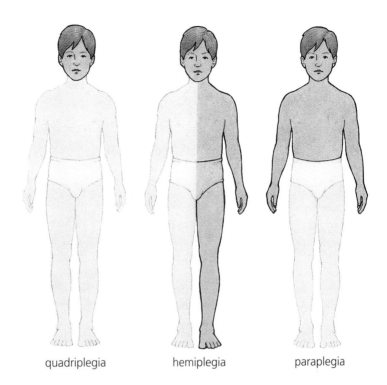

quadriplegia   hemiplegia   paraplegia

In this illustration the parts of the body that no longer receive or transmit signals from the nervous system are faded out. For example, the child demonstrating hemiplegia has lost the use of the right side of his body.

Associations: Paralysis beginning in different parts of the nervous system is associated with different diseases or injuries.

Spinal cord damage: Automobile accidents, accidental falls, and severe sports injuries may involve serious damage to the neck or lower spine that results in paralysis. In these cases the actual cause of the paralysis is a crushed or torn spinal cord. Sometimes other spinal cord conditions, not the direct result of an accident, also can cause paralysis.

Brain damage: Stroke is among the most common causes of paralysis, although stroke victims often regain much or all of the lost function. Brain cancers or even benign tumors in the brain can produce paralysis as a symptom. Parkinson's disease involves the progressive decline of brain cells that control muscles. Cerebral palsy, caused by injury to the brain before, during, or shortly after birth, can result in partial or complete paralysis.

Nerve damage: Poliomyelitis is a viral infection that attacks nerves controlling the muscles and in severe cases causes paralysis. ALS (amyotrophic lateral sclerosis) is a progressive disease of uncertain cause that produces such general paralysis that it is invariably fatal. Botulism, a form of food poisoning, paralyzes chest, arms, and legs along with other symptoms.

Bell's palsy is a paralysis of muscles on one side of the face. Probably caused by an infection of the nerve serving these muscles, this paralysis often lasts no more than a few weeks. It can be permanent, though, leaving the patient with a partially sagging face, drooping mouth, and a tendency to drool from the affected side. Guillain-Barré syndrome can cause paralysis that is usually temporary, although it too can have lingering partial effects.

Brief paralysis is one of the symptoms of narcolepsy; it also is a hallmark of a TIA (transient ischemic attack).

Related symptoms: Depending on the nature of the disorder that caused the paralysis, the patient may experience loss of other bodily or mental functions. Stroke, for example, may cause vision, speech, bowel, bladder, and other problems. A broken neck may not only cause paralysis of the limbs but also affect the patient's ability to breathe independently.

Severe depression often accompanies the onset of paralysis. Losing the ability to walk, for example, or suffering the other debilitating effects of a severe stroke can make a patient extremely despondent, sometimes even to the point of having suicidal thoughts.

Prevention and possible actions: While some types of paralysis are only temporary, people who suffer permanent paralysis of a limb or limbs must undergo extensive rehabilitation. Physical therapy is an essential part of recovery for stroke victims and others who have suffered partial or complete paralysis. The physical therapist, in consultation with the physician, sets up a program of exercises designed to restore muscle function in the affected part when that is possible and to build up other muscles that may be needed to compensate for a permanently paralyzed limb. The therapist may also help the patient learn to use braces, devices that attach to and help support paralyzed limbs. Physical therapists also teach the use of a walker (a movable frame used for extra support while walking), a wheelchair, and special devices such as a powered tricycle or an automobile equipped with controls designed for a handicapped driver.

Researchers have made important strides toward finding out why damaged nerves do not repair themselves and how to make them regenerate. Some think that the use of stem cells or growth factors will someday lead to permanent relief from paralysis.

Paranoia

(paar-uh-NOI-uh)

The classic example of paranoia is a person believing that there is a great conspiracy to do him some harm. He can observe signs of the conspiracy in the most innocent events. Why should this vast effort be made to harm this one man? The man may not be able to say why, exactly, but clearly he thinks it is because he is of supreme importance. Since there is no objective evidence to support his belief—indeed, evidence contradicts such a belief—he suffers from a delusion.

Cause: Paranoia is primarily a symptom of mental illness, but it also results from well-known physical diseases with some mental symptoms. Although paranoia is a common side effect of various chemicals that affect the brain, psychiatrists also recognize that paranoia can exist on its own. For example, a man may fear that he has cancer despite negative tests. His other behavior is rational and appropriate, but he will cling to this belief in the face of all evidence to the contrary.

Recognizing the symptoms: Symptoms similar to paranoia occur in people with no illness. For example, people with paranoia mistrust others. They are quick to take offense and slow to forgive. They attack at the first sign of imagined criticism. They bring many lawsuits. Usually, their mistrust provokes mistrust in others. But such behaviors are also well within the normal range.

Other behaviors, however, are clearly signs of illness. People with paranoia may imagine that everything happening around them has a hidden reference to them. They may imagine secret messages in advertisements or on the T-shirts of people who pass them in the street. They may think family members, coworkers, or others are spying on them. They build complicated plots in their minds that may even seem convincing to others.

Related symptoms: Some paranoid people are so tense that they actually develop physical symptoms, such as tremors, muscular tightness, and cold sweats.

Associations: Paranoia as a symptom is associated with some physical illnesses, such as Alzheimer's disease, Huntington's disease, Parkinson's disease, and stroke. These diseases affect the way that the brain functions, producing mental as well as physical symptoms in various parts of the body.

Paranoia is also associated with mental illnesses. For example, in some cases of clinical depression or bipolar disorder, people who are depressed may feel that they deserve the punishment they imagine is being inflicted on them. Manic patients may also have paranoid symptoms, but they tend more toward the grandiose. Schizophrenia is closely related to paranoia, and a form called paranoid schizophrenia often involves hallucinations, especially the hearing of voices.

Paranoia is often chemically induced. Chronic abuse of cocaine and amphetamines may lead users to develop features of a paranoid personality that may not go away when drug abuse is stopped. Other drugs, such as LSD and mescaline, and even marijuana, may produce instant paranoia. Some people react to drinking alcoholic beverages with paranoid-type symptoms even without other signs of drunkenness; extended alcohol abuse usually produces definite paranoid symptoms. Paranoia is frequently a part of delirium tremens and of the other mental problems that come in late stages of alcoholism. Like the paranoia of extended amphetamine abuse, paranoia that results from years of alcohol abuse may not end with the stoppage of drinking.

Relief of symptoms: Successfully treating an illness that leads to paranoid symptoms often relieves the paranoia as well as other symptoms. Antipsychotic medication can control some symptoms, such as delusions, but the side effects are often unpleasant. Physicians usually prescribe such medications only for short periods to control episodes of extreme agitation, anxiety, or violence.

Individual counseling or psychotherapy may help people break free of paranoia by allowing them to learn the difference between the real and the unreal. Progress is slow and uncertain, however, because people with paranoia are often suspicious of, if not hostile to, therapists. Behavior therapy is treatment that aims at the symptoms instead of the underlying disease. It hopes to reduce a paranoid person's sensitivity to criticism and improve his or her social skills.

Prevention and possible actions: People with paranoia rarely volunteer for treatment. They are seen by mental health professionals only when brought in for care by family or friends.

Types of Paranoia

Paranoia has been classified in a number of different ways. Here are a few of the best known.

Late paranoia occurs in old people who live alone and have few relatives or friends. Their isolation leads to a growing suspicion that others are spying on them or stealing from them. Sometimes these fears are related to other factors in aging, such as failing eyesight or hearing.

In *erotomania* a paranoid person loves another, usually a famous person or someone with higher social standing. The paranoid person is convinced that the famous person is in love as well, but cannot acknowledge it openly. When the paranoid person's love is not returned, he or she feels a sense of betrayal that often turns to hatred and rage. Women with this disorder usually do not act on it, but men frequently find themselves in trouble with the law as a result of pursuing their love interest. *Conjugal paranoia* is extreme jealousy directed at a wife or husband, a variation on erotomania.

In *shared paranoid disorder* a dependent person adopts the delusion of someone he or she is attached to. When separated from the dominant partner, the dependent person can give up the paranoid belief. This disorder usually involves two sisters, a mother and child, or a husband and wife.

In *paranoid schizophrenia* the person has fragmentary and bizarre delusions, or false beliefs along with hallucinations. The schizophrenic may hear voices or think that his or her thoughts are under the control of mysterious powers.

Grandiose delusions need not involve conspiracies; the person with the paranoid idea may simply believe that he or she possesses some great unrecognized importance. *Persecution complex* on the other hand need not involve grandiosity; the persecution may simply be an imagined legal problem.

Parasites and disease

REFERENCE

Any creature that lives at the expense of another is a parasite, but the word *parasite* in medicine refers only to creatures that are more complex than viruses or bacteria. Some one-celled "germs" are parasites. Other parasites that produce diseases in humans are worms of one kind or another. Physicians usually call invasion of the body by a parasite an *infestation*, while invasion by a virus or bacterium is an *infection*.

Parasites often have complicated life cycles. Many must be carried from person to person by another creature, such as a mosquito or other fly. Others live part of their lives in humans and part in another creature, such as a snail or a pig.

Protists: Protists are single-celled organisms. Nearly all are microscopic in size. Although protists used to be thought of as one-celled animals or plants, they are often in between these more familiar types. Sometimes animal-like protists are called *protozoa*. *Algae* are protists, too, but they are often thought of as plants.

Both malaria and the less familiar disease *babesiosis* are caused by protozoan parasites. Malaria and babesiosis are transmitted by bites and have similar symptoms, although malaria is transmitted by tropical mosquitoes, and babesiosis is carried by ticks found throughout the United States. Babesiosis is especially common near the East and West coasts.

Worms: Many different kinds of animals are called worms. About all they have in common is an elongated body. Many of the parasitic worms are flatworms (also called helminths), including flukes and tapeworms. The Guinea worm is a nematode that may be 3 feet long. Worldwide, parasitic worms are thought to infect nearly half the human population. Parasitic worms are difficult for the body to handle, producing only slight immune responses. Thus infestations of worms can last for years or even for life if not treated.

Parasitic insects and arachnids: Insects, such as lice, and arachnids, such as ticks, can become parasites that live largely on the skin instead of within the body. One mite lays its eggs in human skin, causing the skin disease scabies. The main symptom of scabies is an intense itch that is caused when the eggs hatch and baby lice burrow their way out. Other insects and arachnids, such as fleas and chiggers, produce intense itching as well.

In tropical regions of North and South America a small fly called a botfly captures a mosquito or other biting fly and deposits an egg on it. When the mosquito or fly approaches a human or other mammal to feed on it, heat from the mammal's skin causes the egg to hatch. The botfly larva stays with the mammal and burrows into the skin, where it feeds, causing a visible path known as a *warble*.

Treatment options: Parasites are not susceptible to antibiotics, but many types can be killed by chemicals. These chemicals can have powerful side effects and should always be taken under the direction of a physician. Rarely, a parasite may need to be removed by a surgical procedure.

Prevention: For parasitic diseases the best defense comes from avoiding situations in which infestations can occur. Making sure that water is safe to drink is especially important.

A complicated life

Almost all parasites live in or on at least two different kinds of animal during different parts of their lives. Each animal is called a *host* to the parasite.

Many protists live part of their lives in flies of one sort or another; best known is the malaria protist, which lives in mosquitoes. Worms may live in other mammals, in fish, or in snails.

The blacklegged tick lives on meadow mice when it is young, moves to deer to breed, and then waits for another warm-blooded animal on which to feed. Not all parasites need more than one host, however. Some worms live freely in soil and some protists in water until they can reach a human host.

One of the most complicated lives is lived by the fish tapeworm.

7. bear eats large fish tapeworm grows to adult in bear but cannot reproduce or . . .

7. person eats fish; tapeworm grows to adult in human and reproduces

1. egglike stage enters water in human feces

2. hatches

3. grows into adult

4. adult eaten by copepod

5. copepod eaten by small fish, tapeworm lives as parasite in fish

6. larger fish eats small fish, tapeworm moves to larger fish

Many parasites are found primarily in tropical regions, so travelers are at greater risk in such places. Often it helps to drink only bottled water, stay protected against insect bites, and keep skin out of contact with the soil or standing water.

Food and water: Food can be a source of parasites. Meat in the United States that has been inspected by the Agriculture

Diseases caused by protists

Disease, name of protist	Location of infection (size)	Method of transmission
African sleeping sickness, *Trypanosoma brucei*	Blood, lymph system, spinal cord, brain (microscopic)	Bite of tsetse fly
Amebic dysentery, *Entamoeba hystolytica*	Digestive tract (0.004 inch)	In water or on food, especially fresh vegetables
Babesiosis, *Babesia*	Red blood cells (microscopic)	Bite of tick
Chagas' disease, *Trypanosoma cruzi*	Bloodstream (microscopic)	Bite of "Chagas bug" (*Triatoma*)
Cryptosporidiosis, *Cryptosporidium*	Lower intestines (microscopic)	In surface waters, but resistant to chlorination
Cyclospora, *Cyclospora cayetanensis*	Small intestine (microscopic)	In food, especially on fresh fruit
Giardia ("beaver fever"), *Giardia*	Intestinal tract (microscopic)	In flowing water
Leishmaniasis: kala-azar, *Leishmania*	Spleen and intestines (microscopic)	Bite of sandfly
Leishmaniasis: Oriental sore or sandfly fever, *Leishmania*	Skin (microscopic)	Bite of sandfly
Malaria, *Plasmodium*	Blood and liver (microscopic)	Bite of mosquito (*Anopheles*)
Toxoplasmosis, *Toxoplasma gondii*	Intestines, throughout body, fetus	Cat litter, undercooked meat, raw eggs, unpasteurized milk
Trichomonas, *Trichomonas*	Intestines, mouth, birth canal, urinary tract (microscopic)	Sexually from one human to another

Department is nearly always free of tapeworm, but pork can sometimes contain trichinosis. Thorough cooking kills most parasites. Raw fish can also be a source of parasites, although people who prepare raw fish for human consumption are trained to watch for and eliminate infected fish. Ice as well as water can carry some diseases, including amebic dysentery.

Control of agents of transmission: Often the best way known to prevent infection by parasites is to control mosquitoes, snails, deer mice, ticks, and other animals that carry the parasites.

Diseases caused by worms

Disease, name of worm	Location of infection (size)	Method of transmission
Bladder fluke, *Schistosoma haematobium*	Blood vessel of bladder (1.2 inches)	Water inhabited by snails contains larvas that enter through skin
Filariasis, *Wuchereria bancrofti*	Lymph system (3.6 inches)	Mosquito bites
Guinea worm, Dracunculiasis *Dracunculus medinensis*	Abdominal cavity, then female migrates out through skin (30 to 45 inches)	Pain on emergence causes victim to seek cooling water, where eggs are deposited. Larvas ingested by copepods, then released in humans who drink water containing infected copepods
Hookworms (strongyloidiasis), *Ancyclostoma duodenals* **or** *Necator americanus*	Small intestine (0.5 inch) (0.4 inch)	Larvas that live in soil penetrate skin, usually through bare feet
Pinworms, *Enterobius vermicularis*	Colon and rectum (0.4 inch)	Eggs in fecal matter are transmitted to food or objects that are put in mouth
River blindness, *Onchocerca volvulus*	Beneath skin and in the eyes (16 inches)	Bite of tropical black fly
Roundworms, *Ascaris lumbricoides*	Small intestine (8 inches)	Eggs from persons with the disease are shed in fecal matter and are transmitted to food or to objects that are put in the mouth
Schistosomiasis, *Schistosoma mansoni*	Veins, especially in abdomen (0.8 inch)	Water inhabited by tropical snail, *Schistosoma japonica,* contains larvas that enter through skin of persons who bathe in the water
Tapeworm, **Cestoda species, including** *Taenia saginata (beef),* *Taenia solium (pork),* **and** *Dibothriocephalus latus (fish)*	Adult lives in intestines, but larvas may invade other organs (up to 30 feet long)	Eating meat or fish that contains tapeworm larvas; embryos grow in tapeworm segments that are shed in host's fecal matter, from which they infect alternate hosts
Trichinosis, *Trichinella spiralis*	Adults live in small intestine, but larvas form cysts in muscles (0.04 inch)	Pork that contains larval cysts
Whipworm, *Trichuris trichiura*	Part of large intestine called cecum (1.2 inches)	Eggs in fecal matter are transmitted to food or to objects that are put in mouth

Parathyroid glands
(paar-uh-THIY-roid)

BODY SYSTEM

From two to eight parathyroid glands—most often four—are part of the endocrine system. Like the other glands, parathyroids secrete a hormone that helps regulate certain bodily activities. The hormone, called *PTH* (*parathyroid hormone*), regulates the level of calcium in the blood. Adequate calcium is needed for proper functioning of nerves and muscles.

Size and location: Each parathyroid gland is about the size of a pea and lies beside or behind the thyroid gland in the neck.

Role: A drop in blood calcium level stimulates the parathyroid glands to secrete more PTH, causing calcium to be released from the bones, the body's storage area for the mineral. PTH also signals the intestines to increase absorption of calcium from foods and stimulates the kidneys to reabsorb more calcium from urine. If there is too much calcium in the bloodstream, the parathyroids secrete less PTH.

Conditions that affect the parathyroids: *Hyperparathyroidism* usually occurs when one or more of the glands secrete too much PTH. The condition usually affects middle-aged people, especially women (about 6 in 100,000 people). Most often a small, noncancerous tumor growing on a parathyroid gland stimulates the overproduction of PTH. The patient may have no symptoms for quite some time, but eventually the high levels of calcium in the blood cause calcium stones to form in the kidneys. Fatigue may also become a problem, along with indigestion, ulcers, frequent urination, and persistent thirst.

Hyperparathyroidism can also be caused by kidney failure, some bone disorders, and problems with calcium or vitamin D absorption.

Hypoparathyroidism is a fairly rare condition in which a patient has too little calcium in the bloodstream because the parathyroid glands are not producing enough PTH. The low calcium levels lead to such symptoms as muscle twitches, spasms, cramps, and psychological changes. Another frequent symptom is infection by *Candida* yeasts. Accidental damage to parathyroids during surgery on the thyroid is a major cause of this disorder.

Paratyphoid fever
(paar-uh-TIY-foid)

DISEASE

TYPE: INFECTIOUS (BACTERIAL)

Healthcare workers in the twentieth century found that some instances of what appeared to be a milder version of typhoid fever were not caused by *Salmonella typhi*, the bacterium they knew to produce typhoid, so they named the infection paratyphoid fever. Today health authorities outside the United States recognize that several bacteria in the *Salmonella* family cause paratyphoid fever; they term them *Salmonella paratyphi* types A, B, and C. In the United States, however, these bacteria are rare, and the disease they cause is often considered a form of typhoid, although it is also called *salmonellosis*. Veterinarians also label several *Salmonella* infections of birds as paratyphoid fever. Food poisoning is usually caused by different members of the *Salmonella* family.

Cause: Infection is caused by any one of three different types of *Salmonella paratyphi* bacteria. The disease is usually transmitted by the fecal-oral (*enteric*) route, either from persons or animals infected with the disease, although it can sometimes be a form of food poisoning from undercooked meat or egg dishes.

Incidence: Both typhoid and paratyphoid fevers are rare in the United States and other industrial nations. They are more common in Asia and South America.

Noticeable symptoms: There is a characteristic pink rash on the chest or abdomen along with high fever, headache, vomiting, and diarrhea (or sometimes constipation). The rash, known as "rose spots," may develop into small breaks in blood vessels under the skin.

Diagnosis: A characteristic of the disease is an enlarged spleen. Healthcare workers will want to rule out diseases with similar symptoms by culturing the bacteria.

Treatment options: If the cause of the disease is recognized, antibiotics are used to stop the growth of the bacteria. Many *Salmonella* bacteria have developed resistance to several common antibiotics, however, complicating treatment.

Stages and progress: Like typhoid, paratyphoid fever is most often spread by an infected person who does not become ill. Such a person is called a *carrier*. A carrier continually sheds the bacteria in feces, which then become transmitted by poor hygiene to the hands. Unwashed hands can carry the bacteria to food, so food handlers, especially in restaurants, can spread the disease to many people.

Once a susceptible person is infected, the bacteria produce symptoms anywhere from a day to ten days after exposure. The illness usually begins with a high fever followed by symptoms similar to those of gastroenteritis and continuing with a recovery period characterized by weakness and low-grade fever that often lasts several weeks.

Prevention or risk factors: Hand washing and careful handling of food can prevent the spread of this disease. A vaccine is available for those likely to be exposed to the bacteria through travel to countries where typhoid and paratyphoid are more common.

Parkinson's disease

On the Internet
NATIONAL PARKINSON FOUNDATION
www.parkinson.org/site/
pp.asp?c=9dJFJLPwB&b=71125

Parkinson's disease is a serious disease caused by the progressive decline of brain cells responsible for controlling the movement of muscles. It often produces such symptoms as a shaking hand, leg, or head (due to trembling muscles), although not all Parkinson's sufferers develop this characteristic symptom. Also called *shaking palsy,* Parkinson's disease was first recognized in 1817 by the English surgeon James Parkinson.

Cause: Medical researchers still do not know why the brain cells in the substantia nigra (suhb-STAAN-shee-uh NIY-gruh) begin to degenerate in Parkinson's disease. The affected cells stop producing the neurotransmitter *dopamine.* As the disease progresses, less and less dopamine is available in the brain. Since dopamine is involved in transmitting nerve impulses, interference with the brain's control of muscles, centered in this part of the brain, occurs.

Another disorder, called *parkinsonism,* produces symptoms that are essentially the same as those of Parkinson's disease, since dopamine production is also reduced. But parkinsonism is caused by such known factors as head injury, hardening of the arteries in the brain, carbon monoxide poisoning, syphilis, and drug abuse involving an illegal synthetic drug called MPTP, originally intended as a cheap substitute for heroin.

Incidence: Parkinson's disease affects about 1.5 million people in the United States. It usually begins between the ages of 45 and 65, and strikes about 1 in 100 people aged 50 or older.

Noticeable symptoms: The earliest noticeable symptoms may include a slight tremor in the fingers of one hand, the tendency to drag a foot while walking, or stiffness in one of the limbs. Head shaking may become noticeable.

As the disease progresses, it may cause muscle stiffness and rigidity on one or both sides of the body. Stiffness of muscles causes a shuffling gait and rigid facial expression (called "masking"). Tremors disappear when the affected limb is in motion and while the patient sleeps. Fatigue and stress can make tremors worse. More severe cases make walking difficult, and sometimes the disease restricts a patient's mobility almost completely. However, mental capacity is not affected until the later stages, and this occurs in only about a third of all cases.

Diagnosis: Physical examination can reveal stiffness in muscles and a tendency for muscles to react in a jerky manner. Other possible causes for muscle rigidity must be eliminated, however.

Treatment options: Drug therapy is effective. The basic strategy is to provide the brain with the dopamine it no longer produces in adequate amounts by providing levodopa (a precursor to dopamine that becomes dopamine in brain tissue) and by suppressing the mechanisms that reduce dopamine supplies. Over 90% of patients experience an improvement in their symptoms once they begin taking medication; for some the symptoms are almost completely eliminated. But a physician must constantly monitor the patient's condition because the response to medication will vary over time. Side effects such as dizziness, nausea, and changes in the patient's mental state may become pronounced and require a change in dosage.

Other drugs aim at halting tremors by blocking acetylcholine, used in nerve signaling. Botox (botulism toxin) is sometimes used to stop muscle spasms.

Brain surgery is an alternative approach for tremor or spasm control when medications fail. Most commonly, a cut destroys the specific portion of the brain that is affected. The main difficulty with this type of surgery is that the brain cells to be destroyed are very near brain cells that must be retained, such as those in regions of the brain involved in vision. Other forms of brain surgery involve implanting an electronic device that can be activated to halt tremor, and implants of brain tissue from fetal pigs or stem cells from human sources that have been modified to grow into brain cells.

Prevention: Vigorous regular exercise early in adult life cuts a man's risk of Parkinson's in half and also reduces a woman's risk, although not by quite as much. Drinking coffee or caffeinated beverages also seems to reduce risk.

Exercise

Paronychia

See **Nail infections and injuries**

Parrot fever

DISEASE

TYPE: INFECTIOUS
(BACTERIAL)

See also
Animal diseases and humans
Bacteria and disease
Pets and disease
Pneumonia

On the Internet
VICTORIA DEPARTMENT
OF HUMAN SERVICES: BETTER
HEALTH CHANNEL (Australia)
www.betterhealth.vic.gov.au/
bhcv2/bhcarticles.nsf/pages/
Psittacosis_parrot_fever?
OpenDocument

Parrot fever is a disease of the respiratory system. The disease, also called *psittacosis* (SIHT-uh-KOH-sihs) or *ornithosis* (AWR-nuh-THOH-sihs), is transmitted to humans by various birds and domestic fowl, including parrots, parakeets, ducks, chickens, and pigeons. *Psittakos* is Greek for "parrot," while *ornith-* is a combining form meaning "bird."

Cause: The bacterial strain *Chlamydia psittaci,* which infects birds, causes parrot fever in humans. The bird itself may not show any significant signs of illness, but the bacteria are present in the bird's droppings. People get the disease by inhaling bacteria-laden dust from the dried droppings or by handling infected birds.

Incidence: This disease is now rare in the United States; fewer than 50 instances have been recognized in the past five years. Imported parrots and parakeets must be quarantined and fed a diet laced with antibiotics before they can be sold.

Noticeable symptoms: The fever usually appears suddenly and is accompanied by flulike symptoms, including chills, profuse sweating, headache, and cough. If left untreated, difficulty in breathing appears after a week or so with the onset of pneumonia.

Diagnosis: Patients with parrot fever may show signs of lung-tissue inflammation and swelling of the spleen. Blood tests are needed to differentiate this disease from other forms of pneumonia.

Treatment options: Antibiotics such as tetracycline are effective against this disease, especially when medication is begun early.

Prevention: Avoiding contact with dust from bird droppings can help keep a person from contracting the disease.

Patent ductus arteriosus
(PAY-tuhnt DUK-tuhs ahr-TEER-ee-OH-suhs)

DISEASE

TYPE: DEVELOPMENTAL

Two main blood vessels, or arteries, carry blood from the heart to the body. The *pulmonary artery* carries blood to the lungs, where it picks up fresh oxygen. The oxygen-enriched blood then returns to the heart, where it is pumped out through the other main artery, the *aorta,* to the rest of the body.

Before a baby is born and starts breathing air, very little blood is pumped to the not-yet-working lungs. Instead the pul-

See also
Congenital heart defects
Fetus
Heart
Rubella ("German" measles)

On the Internet
TEXAS HEART INSTITUTE
www.tmc.edu/thi/pda.html

Did You Know?

Patent ductus arteriosus occurs in mammals other than humans. It is the most commonly diagnosed congenital heart defect in dogs. Breeds most at risk are the Maltese, Pomeranian, Shetland sheepdog, and Kerry blue terrier.

---

monary artery and the aorta are connected by a passageway called the *ductus arteriosus,* and most of the blood is directed to the rest of the body.

This passageway normally closes within a few days of birth, and circulation to the lungs becomes completely separated from circulation to the rest of the body. But sometimes the passageway remains open, so that some of the blood passing at high pressure through the aorta is forced into the pulmonary artery. The medical term for open is *patent,* so this congenital defect is known as patent ductus arteriosus.

Cause: The cause is unknown. The condition is not hereditary. It is more prevalent among premature babies and those born to mothers who had rubella ("German" measles) during pregnancy.

Incidence: Patent ductus arteriosus is relatively common, occurring in about 8 in 1,000 babies. For reasons that are not known, it affects twice as many girls as boys.

Noticeable symptoms: The diversion of blood can have several harmful effects. Too much blood goes to the lungs, so they become congested with fluid. They work less efficiently and are susceptible to respiratory infections. Too little blood goes to the rest of the body, so the heart must work overly hard to compensate. The turbulent blood flow through the passageway raises the risk of infections in the heart and blood vessels. Children may be pale, easily out of breath, slow to grow, and often sick with a respiratory infection.

Diagnosis: The defect can often be diagnosed at birth by a murmur heard through a stethoscope. X-rays and echocardiography (a form of ultrasound) can be used to confirm the diagnosis.

Treatment options: Sometimes no immediate treatment is necessary. The opening may close by itself. If treatment is needed, a nonsteroidal anti-inflammatory drug (NSAID) such as indomethacin often causes the passage to close. If the drug does not work, the opening can be mechanically sealed in a simple surgical operation.

Pediculosis

See **Lice**

Pellagra

(puh-LAAG-ruh)

DISEASE

TYPE: VITAMIN DEFICIENCY

See also
Alcoholism
Dementia
Diet and health
Starvation and malnutrition
Vitamin-deficiency diseases

> **Did You Know?**
> Francisco Frapolli of Italy gave this disease its name in 1771, from *pelle* (skin) and *agra* (rough), on the basis of its characteristic rash.

A potentially serious disorder, pellagra can be caused by a diet that lacks enough foods containing either the vitamin niacin (NIY-uh-sihn—also known as vitamin B_3) or the amino acid tryptophan (TRIHP-tuh-FAAN), which the body uses to synthesize niacin. Maize (corn) is low in these nutrients, and a diet based on corn can lead to the disease.

Cause: In addition to a dietary deficiency pellagra can also be brought on by chronic alcoholism and by drug addiction, each of which interferes with the metabolism of B vitamins. Poor absorption of nutrients from other diseases can have pellagra as a side effect.

Incidence: Once the most widespread form of vitamin deficiency in the southeastern United States—in 1930 some 5,000 women and 2,000 men died from the disease—pellagra later declined sharply, thanks to public health programs. Since 1980 American deaths from pellagra have essentially been zero. The disease continues to strike elsewhere during famines and war.

Noticeable symptoms: Early symptoms are fairly mild, including an inflamed tongue, soreness of the mouth, skin problems, irritability, diarrhea, loss of appetite, and weight loss. Patients soon suffer red, dry, scaly skin lesions in areas exposed to sunlight, such as the back of the hands or where clothing chafes against the skin. The mouth may become inflamed, with sores developing near the mouth as well.

The mental problems begin with insomnia and irritability. If the niacin deficiency persists, more severe symptoms appear, including memory loss, hallucinations, and violent and irrational behavior.

Pellagra was once known as the disease of the four D's—dermatitis, diarrhea, dementia, and death.

Treatment options: Niacin given orally is an effective way to treat pellagra in the short term, although an improved diet is considered preferable for long-term treatment, along with reduced alcohol consumption when necessary.

Niacin supplements in high doses, which sometimes are used to lower blood cholesterol, may cause liver damage or irregular heartbeat; large amounts of niacin should be taken only under a physician's care.

Prevention: Eating a balanced diet containing foods high in niacin offers the best protection against this vitamin-deficiency disease. Good sources of niacin include liver, lean meats, fish, peanuts, and whole-grain cereals. Milk and eggs, while low in niacin, contain tryptophan, which the body can use to synthesize niacin.

Heavy alcohol consumption increases the need for niacin. The amount in ordinary doses of B-complex vitamins may be helpful for alcohol abusers.

Penis

BODY SYSTEM

See also
Cancers
Diabetes mellitus, type 1
Diabetes mellitus, type 2
Erectile dysfunction
Genital herpes
Gonorrhea
Reproductive system
STD (sexually transmitted diseases)
Syphilis
Testes
Trichomonas
Warts

Male humans possess a multipurpose external organ called the penis. It contains the *urethra*, which is the tube used for expelling urine from the body (in a female human the urethra is in the abdomen). That same male urethra is the passage for sperm-containing semen during copulation.

Size and location: Although the penis normally is soft and flexible, it needs to be hard and stiff to enter a woman's vagina during copulation. To achieve this transformation, called *erection*, the penis is made from three different masses of spongy tissue filled with many blood vessels. During erection, which can take place spontaneously (usually during sleep) or when there is sexual stimulation, the arteries enlarge to admit more blood while the veins shut down to keep the blood in the penis. Fluid pressure produces the erection.

Before erection a typical adult penis is about four inches long; during erection it is about six inches long. Boys are born with extra skin covering the tip of the penis. Often this *foreskin* is removed a few days after birth (*circumcision*).

Role: During copulation muscular contractions at the end of the process expel about a teaspoonful or two of semen, which can contain as many as 500 million sperm. If there are fewer than about 150 million, fertilization seldom occurs.

Conditions that affect the penis: Certain sexually transmitted diseases, especially syphilis and genital herpes, often have a

Phone doctor

sore on the exterior of the penis as an early symptom. Uncircumcised men, especially those with diabetes, are likely to develop infections under the foreskin or other foreskin-related problems. Warts may be sexually transmitted or simply develop on the penis. *Because cancer and syphilitic sores can resemble warts, consult a physician about any growth on the penis.* Do not use over-the-counter wart treatments on the penis as its thin and sensitive skin is easily damaged. Cancer of the penis is rare, but does occur.

Other sexually transmitted infections, such as gonorrhea or trichomonas, are primarily located inside the urethra. Often the cause of infection of the urethra is unknown and may be labeled *nonspecific urethritis* by a physician. Infection of the urethra can result in blockage, known as *urethral stricture;* this is corrected by scraping the interior of the urethra.

Inability to achieve erection is termed impotence or *erectile dysfunction*. A curved erection (*Peyronie's disease*) often resolves itself, but sometimes surgery is needed to correct the condition. Sometimes an erection begins and will not go away, a condition called *priapism* (PRIY-aa-pihz-uhm). *This painful condition is a serious disorder that requires emergency treatment.* If not corrected within three or four hours, priapism can cause permanent impotence.

Emergency Room

Peptic ulcers

See **Ulcers**

Pericarditis

(PEHR-ih-kaar-DIY-tihs)

DISEASE

TYPE: INFLAMMATION

Pericarditis is an inflammation of the *pericardium* (PEHR-ih-KAAR-dee-uhm), the thin membrane that covers the heart. Because the heart constantly beats, pushing against the inflamed tissue, pain is nearly constant.

Cause: *Acute pericarditis* is usually caused by a viral infection. It may also occur in association with arthritis, lupus, rheumatic fever, chronic kidney failure, cancer, or other diseases. Rarely, it is caused by a serious chest injury or a heart attack. *Chronic constrictive pericarditis* may be caused by tuberculosis, radiation therapy, or heart surgery.

Phone doctor

On the Internet

INTELIHEALTH

www.intelihealth.com/IH/ihtIH/
WSIHW000/9339/24447.html

Incidence: Pericarditis occurs in people of all ages. Acute pericarditis is most common in adult men under the age of 50.

Noticeable symptoms: The main symptom is severe pain in the center of the chest that may spread to the neck and left shoulder. It becomes worse when lying down or breathing in deeply. There is usually a dry cough. Acute pericarditis may also be accompanied by fever, chills, and weakness.

In chronic constrictive pericarditis the pericardium thickens and stiffens. This causes the pericardium to shrink and constrict the heart and makes it difficult for the heart to fill with blood. This may produce symptoms that include shortness of breath and fluid buildup in the legs, abdomen, or lungs. ***Consult your physician if you have any of these symptoms.***

Diagnosis: The physician will listen for a rubbing sound when a stethoscope is placed over your heart; in later stages heart sounds weaken. A CT scan or MRI (magnetic resonance image) of the chest will reveal any thickening of the pericardium.

Treatment options: Bed rest and painkillers or anti-inflammatory drugs are usually the only treatment required. Antibiotics or antifungal medicines may be used when appropriate. When there is fluid accumulation around the heart, a needle may be inserted into the pericardial sac to remove the fluid. The pericardium may have to be surgically removed in cases of extreme constrictive pericarditis.

Periodontal disease

(PEHR-ee-uh-DON-tuhl)

DISEASE

TYPE: INFECTIOUS (BACTERIAL)

Periodontal disease is the second most common dental disorder after tooth decay. *Periodontal* means "around the teeth," and periodontal disease affects the gums and other tissues in which the teeth are embedded. The disease usually starts with gingivitis—gum inflammation—but it may eventually progress to *periodontitis*—sometimes called *pyorrhea* (PIY-uh-REE-uh)—in which the gums and underlying tooth sockets in the jawbones are damaged.

Cause: Like tooth decay, periodontal disease is believed to result mainly from the bacteria in plaque and its hardened by-

See also
Bacteria and disease
Dental illnesses and conditions
Gingivitis
Teeth

On the Internet
AMERICAN ACADEMY
OF PERIODONTOLOGY
www.perio.org/consumer/2a.html

Did You Know?
Dental floss of some sort was used by prehistoric humans, but the modern practice of regular flossing began after 1819 and commercial dental floss first appeared in 1896.

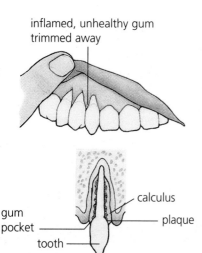

inflamed, unhealthy gum trimmed away

gum pocket

calculus

plaque

tooth

Gum disease results in loose teeth and often produces general ill health as well. Deep pockets of infection along the roots of teeth erode the jawbone in which teeth are embedded.

product *calculus* (or *tartar*). These bacteria release toxins that cause gingivitis, which may lead to periodontitis, especially if untreated.

Incidence: Periodontal disease is the most common cause of tooth loss in adults.

Noticeable symptoms: Periodontal disease begins with swelling and redness, often accompanied by bleeding. This stage may or may not be painful. In advanced periodontitis teeth may become loose in their sockets.

Diagnosis: A dentist or periodontist (a specialist in gum disorders) measures the depth of hollow pockets containing eroded gum tissue where the gums meet the teeth. Deeper pockets mean more serious periodontal disease. If the tooth sockets become eroded, x-rays will reveal the damage to the bone.

Treatment options: Treatment is determined by how far the disease has progressed. When pockets form, the periodontist or a dental technician uses an ultrasonic cleaner or a small hand instrument called a scaler to remove plaque and tartar from the roots below the gum line. Then the root surfaces are planed smooth, so that the gums can heal and reattach.

If the gums are so badly damaged that they will not heal on their own, it may be necessary to remove diseased tissue by "flap" surgery. Under local anesthesia the inner sides of the pockets are cut away, and the remaining loose flaps of gum are sewn tight against the teeth.

If the tooth sockets have become eroded and the teeth are loose, they may be stabilized with a dental splint. A temporary splint may be made of wire wrapped around the bases of the teeth so that they support one another. A more permanent splint is composed of a metal bar embedded along the inner sides of the teeth.

Prevention: The best way to prevent periodontal disease is good oral hygiene—daily brushing and flossing backed up by regular visits to a dentist for cleaning. Since gum inflammation often starts in the spaces between the teeth, regular flossing to remove plaque in these areas is especially important.

Peripheral artery disease

On the Internet
FAMILY DOCTOR
familydoctor.org/008.xml

Did You Know?
Walking after leg-muscle pain develops is harmful to the muscles, but resting until pain stops and then resuming walking develops blood vessels and eventually reduces peripheral artery disease in legs.

Peripheral artery disease (PAD), also called peripheral vascular disease, is characterized by narrowed arteries throughout the body. Its most common sign is cramps in both calves after walking a short distance. The pain goes away when walking stops, but resumes after another few blocks of walking. This symptom is called intermittent claudication.

Cause: Narrowed arteries are commonly caused by fatty deposits on the lining of the arteries. Such deposits result from high levels of cholesterol in blood. Arteries are also narrowed by nicotine.

Incidence: In the United States, some 12 million persons are thought to have PAD. Many of them are undiagnosed. Aging is a major factor, with most instances among people over 40.

Noticeable symptoms: Intermittent claudication results from too little oxygen reaching leg muscles, which use more oxygen when working. Other symptoms of poor blood circulation include brittle nails, scaly skin, and poor healing of wounds, especially wounds on the lower part of the leg. A physician diagnoses PAD by listening to blood flow with a stethoscope, by using a form of ultrasound, or by comparing blood pressure in different parts of the body. Often all three tests are needed to confirm PAD.

Prevention and treatment: Lifestyle changes that help prevent PAD from developing are also a principal form of treatment—stopping smoking, eating a low-fat diet, and exercising regularly. Most cases of intermittent claudication can be resolved by walking for at least 30 minutes a day at least three times a week. The patient walks until pain becomes too great to keep going, rests until the pain goes away, and then walks again.

If lifestyle changes and walking are not sufficient, drugs that lower cholesterol, such as the statins, are helpful, as are medicines that promote circulation, especially cilostazol (Pletal) and clopidogrel (Plavix). Resistant cases can be treated with angiography (inflating a small balloon inside an artery to widen it) or surgery to replace a narrowed artery with a section of vein.

Certain diseases have PAD as one of their symptoms, including diabetes mellitus and hypertension. Managing these diseases will not cure PAD, but well-managed diabetes is less likely to cause leg sores that heal badly or not at all.

Peritonitis

(PEHR-ih-tuh-NIY-tihs)

DISEASE

TYPE: INFECTIOUS
(BACTERIAL)

Emergency Room

See also
Appendicitis
Bacteria and disease
Dehydration
Diverticular diseases
Gonorrhea
Heart failure
PID (pelvic inflammatory disease)
Shock
Spleen

The wall of the abdomen—the part of the trunk below the diaphragm, sometimes called the belly—and the organs within the abdomen are covered with a two-layered membrane called the *peritoneum*. Peritonitis is an inflammation of the peritoneum. It may be localized or it may be present throughout the abdominal cavity.

Cause: Peritonitis is most often caused by bacteria that have invaded the abdominal cavity. Usually, this occurs as the result of a ruptured (burst) organ, such as a ruptured appendix or spleen. These organs can burst open because of internal pressure from pus and bacterial action. Stab wounds and surgery also may introduce bacteria into the cavity.

Noticeable symptoms: The main symptom is severe abdominal pain, most intense in the region of the underlying cause—near a ruptured appendix, for example. Nausea, vomiting, abdominal tenderness, chills, fever, rapid breathing, and rapid pulse are other symptoms. Left untreated, peritonitis can cause dehydration, shock, heart failure, and death. Therefore, *it is important to seek medical help as soon as possible.*

Diagnosis: A physician will admit you to a hospital, where x-rays and blood tests will be used to confirm the diagnosis. A small incision may be made into the abdominal cavity to remove some of the fluid and bacteria to determine their origin.

Treatment options: Treatment involves three basic steps:

- The ruptured tissue that allowed bacteria to enter the abdominal cavity must be surgically repaired.
- The infection must be eliminated; this is usually done with antibiotics.
- Body fluids and chemicals lost during the attack must be replaced; this is usually done with intravenous fluids. Blood transfusions may be needed if the patient is in shock.

Blood pressure, urine flow, and other vital signs will be monitored regularly, and steps will be taken to prevent respiratory problems. Morphine or another painkiller may be administered. The patient will be fed intravenously for at least two days.

Pernicious anemia

See **Anemias**

Pertussis
(puhr-TUS-ihs)

DISEASE

TYPE: INFECTIOUS
(BACTERIAL)

See also
Bacteria and disease
Coughs
Infants and disease
Pneumonia
Vaccination and disease

On the Internet
KIDS HEALTH
kidshealth.org/parent/
infections/bacterial_viral/
whooping_cough.html

Both children and adults may contract pertussis, commonly known as *whooping cough*. The "whoop" is a sudden gasping sound from deep within the chest that accompanies the cough in infants. Older people may have the cough without the whoop, so they may not recognize that they have pertussis.

Cause: The bacterium *Bordetella pertussis* causes pertussis. Infection causes the airways of the lungs to fill up with mucus, making breathing difficult.

Incidence: Pertussis tends to strike infants before vaccination, unvaccinated children and adults, and older children or adults whose immunity has begun to wear off. It is cyclical with higher rates of infection every three to four years.

Recently, there has been a rise in incidence, probably due to unvaccinated children and older persons whose childhood vaccinations are no longer effective. There were more than 25,000 reported cases in 2004 in the United States, up from a low of 1,010 in 1976. Anyone over the age of 12 who has not had booster shots may develop the disease.

Pertussis is frequently overlooked in adults. Many adults with coughs are found to have the disease when tested for pertussis bacteria. Thus it is thought that total incidence in the population is underreported.

Noticeable symptoms: The early signs are easy to dismiss as those of a normal cold—fever, cough, and runny nose. Fever will most likely be present the first week. However, the cough becomes more severe and remains for many weeks. Coughing spells are prolonged, lasting up to a minute in children but less in adults. Children may also vomit after coughing. Headaches, sinus pain, and attacks of sneezing, sweating, or choking are more common in adults than in children.

Diagnosis: The characteristic cough in children is the symptom that physicians recognize. The absence of whooping in adults makes the disease more difficult to diagnose. A sample of the mucus of an infected person or a blood test will show the presence of the *Bordetella pertussis* bacteria.

Treatment options: The disease is treated with antibiotics, which seldom result in a cure but usually reduce the intensity and frequency of coughing. However, the cough may continue in a less severe form after antibiotic therapy ends. Doctors seldom prescribe a cough suppressant during pertussis. A cough helps get the excess mucus out of the lungs, preventing further complications.

Most children can be cared for at home during the time they have pertussis, although infants less than a year and a half old need to be watched constantly because they sometimes stop breathing. On some occasions a baby or child may need to be hospitalized. This is usually done when the coughing is severe and oxygen is needed to help the child breathe.

Stages and progress: After the bacteria enter the body, it takes between 7 and 14 days for the symptoms to start. When the disease first appears, it is mild. As it progresses, the coughing becomes severe and can cause the patient to turn deep red or even blue. This very serious sign of lack of oxygen is called *hypoxia*. If untreated this condition can be deadly. The coughing can be severe for two to ten weeks. After this time the coughing can last for months, but in a milder form. The coughing can cause a rare complication of pertussis—breaking of a blood vessel in the head. There is also the potential for pneumonia because of the overproduction of mucus clogging the lungs.

Get vaccinated

Prevention: Children are vaccinated with five DTaP shots (diphtheria, tetanus, and pertussis) before the age of six, starting at six months of age. Immunization of infants continues to be the best defense. The main danger is to an infant exposed to the disease before vaccination.

Research indicates that pertussis vaccine lasts for a limited amount of time; hence the increase of the disease in adolescents and adults. Adults or teenagers should use a booster vaccine called Td or Tdap (which also protects against tetanus) starting around the age of 11 or 12 and then every 10 years thereafter.

Pets and disease

On the Internet
CENTERS FOR DISEASE CONTROL
AND PREVENTION (CDC):
HEALTHY PETS HEALTHY PEOPLE
www.cdc.gov/healthypets/
index.htm

Pets, from dogs and cats to turtles and spiders, are animals people harbor and feed because they want them around. Studies have shown that keeping pets improves mental health for their owners and contributes to recovery from disease. Sometimes, however, the close contact between pets and humans leads to disease. Even though pets *can* transmit diseases to humans, they rarely do. Most diseases that pets get cannot be transmitted to humans—and vice versa. However, there are about 30 diseases that humans can catch from pets, either directly or from other animals that use pets as transport to people. *Zoonosis* (zoh-ON-uh-sihs) is the name for any disease that can be caught from animals, including pets. Some of these diseases are mild, but a few can be fatal.

Dogs and cats: By far the most common pets are dogs and cats.

The most serious illness that can be transmitted by pet dogs or cats is rabies, a disease of the nervous system that is always fatal if not treated early. Rabies occurs naturally among small wild mammals such as raccoons, bats, skunks, foxes, and armadillos. Pets can contract rabies after having been bitten or scratched by an infected wild animal. When an animal becomes ill from rabies, it is infectious. In the United States most dogs and cats are by law regularly vaccinated against rabies. As a result the average for human rabies in the United States is less than one case per year. In countries that do not require pet immunization for rabies, human cases are more common.

Allergy is the most frequent human illness related to cats and dogs. Many people are allergic to dander, loose flakes of skin shed along with animal fur. In some people these allergies can be life-threatening, so for those a different kind of pet would be a better choice.

Dogs and cats that spend time outdoors can bring home minuscule hitchhikers that carry diseases. Tiny ticks that may be too small to be seen easily can carry Lyme disease, ehrlichiosis, babesiosis, and Rocky Mountain spotted fever. The ticks attach to the pet's fur and are carried into the house. Some ticks bite and attach to the pet, potentially causing infection in the animal. Others transfer to humans as they play with and care for the pet. The ticks can then cause human illnesses.

Fleas are another pet hitchhiker. They can cause painful, itchy bites to both humans and pets. In places where plague is found in wild animals, such as certain areas of the American Southwest, the fleas may carry and transmit this disease.

Intestinal parasites of cats and dogs can also be transmitted to humans when good pet and human hygiene is not maintained. Young pets especially can be infested with roundworms and tapeworms. Tiny eggs are eliminated from the body with the feces, so contact with feces can transmit the parasites to humans. Women who are or who might be pregnant and people with weakened immune systems run special risks from cat feces. Cat feces can carry the parasite that causes toxoplasmosis. Infections of this disease in a pregnant woman result in slight or no symptoms for her. But her infection may be passed through the placenta to the fetus. This infection can also cause serious illness in a person with a weakened immune system. Regular veterinary checkups can catch and treat parasite infections early, protecting the health of both the pet and the owner.

Hair loss in dogs can signal allergies in the pet or a ringworm infestation. When it is the latter, the fungus that causes ringworm can infect the skin of the person caring for the pet and transmit the disease.

Cats can also transmit a disease called cat-scratch fever. This mostly infects children and seems most prevalent in the cold weather months, when children are often indoors with their cats.

Diseases transmitted by other pets: Parakeets and other birds kept as pets do not present as many disease hazards to humans as cats and dogs do. Parrots and parakeets imported into the United States undergo both a quarantine period and antibiotic treatment, so they are seldom the cause of parrot fever these days. However, any bird, not just a parrot, can transmit parrot fever, which has flulike symptoms. Pet birds, which normally stay inside, are unlikely to be exposed to avian influenza ("bird flu"). *Cryptosporidium*, an intestinal parasite, can sometimes be transmitted by pet birds to their owners.

Small mammals, including hamsters, guinea pigs, gerbils, and rabbits, pose virtually no health risks to their owners other than allergies and rare infections from bites or scratches.

Pets comfort humans in many ways, including improving the human's mental health, but they can carry diseases that harm humans as well. The hair and dander from a long-haired cat often provokes allergies. Even a well-cared-for cat can inflict cat-scratch fever with its claws and expose vulnerable persons to toxoplasmosis. Cats that live inside the house at all times, however, are unlikely to expose humans to dangerous diseases, such as those carried by ticks.

Wash hands

Reptiles have been associated with the transmission of bacterial diseases such as salmonella. In some places turtles have been such regular carriers of bacteria that they have been banned from commerce. People who keep snakes as pets expose themselves to snakebite; rarely, a large constrictor kept as a pet will attack its owner.

Pet fish, insects, and spiders are not subject to diseases that affect humans, nor are they likely to inflict damage from bites. The popular tarantula spider looks more dangerous than it is, for example, although some are allergic to its venom.

Prevention: Simple hygiene and sensible caution are generally enough to protect against diseases families might catch from pets. Supervising a pet's outdoor activities can reduce harmful contacts with wild animals. Regular grooming is an opportunity to find and remove ticks, to check for flea infestations, and to identify skin conditions such as ringworm early. Grooming also removes loose fur that can cause allergic reactions. Keeping a cat's claws well clipped can reduce hazards from scratching. Treating a pet humanely, with no teasing or threatening, can reduce biting and scratching behaviors. Proper disposal of pet wastes reduces the risk of transmission of intestinal parasites. Regular cleaning of the pet's sleeping area also reduces the risk of disease transmission. Regular veterinary checkups and immunizations protect the pet's human family from most of the serious illnesses that are transmitted from pets to people.

An important way humans can protect themselves from pet-transmitted diseases is to wash their hands frequently. It is a good idea to wash your hands after petting or grooming a pet, after cleaning up a pet's wastes, and before eating or other activity where there will be hand contact to the mouth, eyes, or face. People at high risk for parasite infection, such as pregnant women and those with weakened immune systems, should consider having someone else change cat litter or clean bird cages. If this is not an option, wearing a mask and putting on latex gloves are effective in preventing transmission. People with pet allergies who choose to have pets should regularly clean both their own and the pet's living areas to reduce allergens. In severe cases they may want to consider allergy shots to reduce their reaction to their pet.

Phagocytes and other leukocytes

(FAAG-uh-sɪʏтᴢ) (LOO-kuh-sɪʏтᴢ)

BODY SYSTEM

See also

Allergies

Autoimmune diseases

Blood

Cancers

Hodgkin's disease

Immune system

Leukemia

Lymphocytes

Neutropenia

**SCID (severe combined
immunodeficiency)**

There are many cells produced as part of the immune system by the bone marrow. These are often grouped under the general heading *white blood cells* although the medical term for these white blood cells is *leukocytes*. There are two main types of leukocytes: *granulocytes* ("grain-containing cells") and *agranulocytes* ("cells without grains"), divisions based on how cells appear through a microscope. The most famous are the main kinds of agranulocytes, the lymphocytes, which are covered in a separate entry. Inflammation is controlled by the other agranulocytes, called *monocytes* (MON-uh-siytz) or *macrophages*. The macrophage was the first leukocyte to come to the attention of scientists, caught in the act of apparently eating a bacterium.

Leukocytes that ingest bacteria, dead cells, and other small foreign materials are called *phagocytes,* or "eater cells." Other leukocytes help protect the body by releasing proteins involved in allergic reactions, ranging from *interferons* to *histamines.*

Neutrophils are small granulocyte phagocytes. They get their name, which means "loves neutral," from the neutral dye that stains them. *Mast cells* collect near a source of infection and release histamines, which cause phagocytes to gather and quell the infection. Two smaller granulocytes that also use chemical warfare against infection are *eosinophils* (EE-uh-SIHN-uh-fihlz) and *basophils* (BAY-suh-fihlz).

Size and location: All white blood cells are microscopic, although the macrophages ("big eaters") are considerably larger than the others. Normally each milliliter of blood contains

When a phagocyte ingests an invader, it stimulates a lymphocyte to begin making antibodies. The next time a similar invader arrives, the lymphocyte system is already primed for action against it.

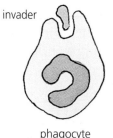
invader

phagocyte

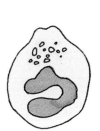

lymphocyte

antibodies

from 5,000 to 10,0000 leukocytes, with numbers rising higher when fighting an infection.

Although the leukocytes are found in blood, they are also common in lymph and in the fluid between cells. They often leave the blood and lymph capillaries to reach the source of an infection.

Role: When an antibody binds to a protein, it attracts a macrophage, which proceeds to "eat" the protein and anything attached to it, such as a cell, thus removing the whole complex. The macrophage, after eating a cell, pushes the original protein that triggered the antibody to its own surface, where the protein projects from the macrophage cell membrane and causes lymphocytes to make antibodies against it.

Allergic reactions include enlargement of blood vessels to bring more phagocytes into action, contraction of airways, and fever. Some two dozen chemicals called interferons, released mostly by the leukocytes, fine-tune operations of the immune system. Some chemicals released by leukocytes kill cells near them.

These reactions not only protect the body against bacteria, viruses, and other parasites, but also fight the development of tumors.

Conditions that affect the leukocytes: The primary diseases are cancers or cancerlike conditions known as leukemias. Although Hodgkin's disease affects the macrophages, it may be a disease essentially of the lymphatic system, not of the leukocytes.

Sometimes a reaction to medication destroys the neutrophils, a condition known as neutropenia. Genetic flaws can render useless several different parts of the immune system, resulting in SCID (severe combined immunodeficiency).

When the system is improperly tuned, the leukocytes may attack perfectly healthy tissue, producing an autoimmune disease.

Pharyngitis	*See* **Sore throat**
Pheochromocytoma	*See* **Hormone disorders**
Phlebitis	*See* **Thrombophlebitis**

PID (pelvic inflammatory disease)

DISEASE

TYPE: INFECTIOUS
(BACTERIAL)

Phone doctor

See also
Bacteria and disease
Fallopian tubes
Gonorrhea
Menstrual pain
Ovaries
Reproductive system
STD (sexually transmitted diseases)
Uterus
Vaginitis

The most common complication of sexually transmitted diseases in women is PID (pelvic inflammatory disease).

Cause: Almost any bacteria can cause PID but the most common causes are chlamydia or gonorrhea, both of which are sexually transmitted. The bacteria migrate from the vagina into the uterus, fallopian tubes, ovaries, and even the abdominal cavity. PID usually develops from two days to three weeks after exposure.

Incidence: The highest rates of PID are among sexually active teenagers. Each year, more than 1 million U.S. teens and adult women are treated for PID; 200,000 to 300,000 of them require hospitalization. Incidence is higher in countries where access to health care is poor.

Noticeable symptoms: Lower abdominal pain, abnormal discharge from the vagina, fever, painful intercourse, and irregular menstrual periods can signal PID.

Diagnosis: A physician will perform an examination and may take a smear of vaginal discharge to identify bacteria present. Additional tests may be necessary.

Treatment options: Treatment should begin promptly to minimize the risk of irreversible, long-term complications. PID is treated with antibiotics. The full course of antibiotics must be taken, even if symptoms go away. Since bacteria are passed between partners during sex, both partners should be treated with antibiotics at the same time. In the most serious cases of PID, surgery may be needed to remove damaged tissue.

Prevention: The best prevention for PID is to avoid sexually transmitted diseases by using a condom during sex. If a sexually transmitted disease is suspected, be certain that it is diagnosed and treated quickly and effectively. Some public health professionals recommend routine screening and treatment for chlamydia infection in all sexually active women even when no symptoms are present.

Pimples

See **Acne**

Pineal gland

(PIHN-ee-uhl)

Although it appears to be similar to other endocrine glands, the pineal gland has long been thought by mystics to be more important. But the only definite role known for the gland is regulation of sleep cycles. Nevertheless, much remains unknown about the gland and considerable research continues on its importance to other life processes, including reproduction and aging.

Size and location: A tiny pine-cone shaped organ, the pineal gland is located deep inside the brain, under the cerebrum and just above the cerebellum. Fairly small, the gland is only about a quarter of an inch long in an adult and may range from a white to pinkish gray color. Location in the brain is thought by some to mean that the pineal and the similarly located pituitary gland are mediators between mental or emotional states and physical ones.

Role: Scientists do not fully understand the gland's role in humans although they know it secretes a hormone called *melatonin* (MEHL-uh-TOH-nihn). It is also involved in production of the neurotransmitter *serotonin* (SEHR-uh-TOH-nihn), known to affect mood in humans. Studies have shown that the pineal gland in animals has a role in sexual development, breeding cycles, and hibernation.

The pineal gland is sometimes called the "third eye." Although in humans it does not receive light directly, it does receive signals from the eye via a circuitous path through the different parts of the brain. Recognition of light and dark is important, since the pineal appears to control the body's biological time clock, maintaining its 24-hour cycles (circadian rhythm). Melatonin production in humans is greatest at night, and injection of the hormone has been shown to make people sleepy.

The pineal gland seems to play an important role in human sexual development. The large quantity of melatonin it secretes during early childhood is believed to somehow delay or slow a child's sexual development. Children also need more sleep because of this excess melatonin.

Melatonin's effect on the sex hormones testosterone and estrogen results from its control of the pituitary's production of luteinizing hormone (LH).

Conditions that affect the pineal gland: Both *benign* and *cancerous tumors* may develop on the pineal gland. The pineal gland has also been linked to SAD (seasonal affective disorder), which leaves some people depressed during the long winter months. Doctors believe the depression develops because people are exposed to less sunlight during winter. Sunlight reduces secretions by the pineal gland.

Pink eye

DISEASE

TYPE: COMBINATION

Phone doctor

See also
Allergies
Bacteria and disease
Eyes and vision
Trachoma
Viruses and disease

On the Internet
MAYO CLINIC
www.mayoclinic.com/health/
pink-eye/DS00258

Pink eye, or *conjunctivitis* (kuhn-JUNGK-tuh-VIY-tihs), is an inflammation of the membranes that cover the white of the eye and line the eyelid. Pink eye is usually not dangerous. But other conditions bearing initial symptoms similar to those of pink eye can cause blindness, so **consult your physician if symptoms are severe or persistent, or if vision is impaired.**

Cause: Pink eye can be caused by infections, both bacterial and viral, by allergies, or by chemical irritants.

Incidence: Children are particularly susceptible to bacterial and viral conjunctivitis. Adults may also suffer occasionally, usually from allergic or chemical conjunctivitis.

Noticeable symptoms: Red eyes are common to all types of pink eye. A thick, sticky discharge that causes the eyelids to stick together at wakening indicates bacterial conjunctivitis. A profuse watery discharge and swelling without pain often can be identified as viral conjunctivitis. Allergic and chemical conjunctivitis symptoms are similar to those of viral conjunctivitis with the addition of pronounced itching and swelling of the eyelids.

Diagnosis: If infection is suspected, a physician may take a swab of the discharge to determine the specific cause. This is particularly true when treating newborn babies, who occasionally acquire some bacterial or viral infection from the mother during passage through the birth canal.

Treatment options: Bacterial infections are treated with antibiotic eyedrops or ointment. Viral infections typically resolve on their own, although that may take a week or more. Allergic or chemically induced pink eye, triggered by exposure to pollen, contact lens solutions, and eye makeup, may be relieved by antihistamines.

Get vaccinated

Prevention: A person with viral or bacterial pink eye may infect others easily. Frequent hand washing and temporary isolation from others help prevent the infection's spread. The infected person should not share linens, toys, eyedroppers, or makeup. Several common causes of pink eye can be prevented by the normal course of vaccinations.

Pinworms

DISEASE

TYPE: PARASITIC

See also
Infants and disease
Parasites and disease

On the Internet
AMERICAN ACADEMY OF FAMILY PHYSICIANS
familydoctor.org/139.xml

> **Did You Know?**
> A female pinworm can produce more than 10,000 eggs. After laying her eggs, she dies.

Pinworm infestation is a common and annoying condition, but generally it is not serious.

Cause: Pinworms (*Enterobius vermicularis*) are tiny worms about one-third of an inch long that look like white threads. Pinworm eggs must be swallowed to cause infestation. They can be passed from anus to hands to mouth when there is poor bathroom hygiene. Pinworms enter the body when their eggs are ingested with food contaminated by contact with dirty hands or when dirty hands touch the mouth. The eggs hatch in the lower intestine, and the worms make their homes there, with some crawling out through the anus during the night to lay eggs.

Incidence: Pinworms most commonly affect preschool and school-aged children. Frequently, when a child is affected, other family members are affected as well.

Noticeable symptoms: A person infected with pinworms will experience anal itching, irritability, and sleeplessness. Women may have itching in the external genital area. There is often a sensation of something crawling around the anal area.

Diagnosis: If a doctor suspects pinworms in a child, the physician will have the parents apply a piece of transparent tape between the buttocks near the anus. When the child first awakes, the tape is removed carefully and placed sticky side down on a microscope slide. The physician will examine the slide looking for pinworm eggs. This procedure may be repeated for several days.

Treatment options: Antiparasite medicine taken orally is effective in treating pinworms. In some cases all members of the family need to be treated. Bedding, clothing, and toys should be laundered thoroughly to destroy any eggs that may be on them.

Stages and progress: Pinworm eggs can live outside the body for two weeks. Inside the body the eggs hatch and the worms live in the lower intestine. At night they come out of the anus and lay their eggs between the buttocks.

Prevention: Good hand washing after bathroom use is the best way to prevent the spread of pinworms. Keeping a child's fingernails short prevents eggs from getting under the nails. Frequent laundering of bedclothes and frequent vacuuming will also reduce the spread of pinworm eggs.

Wash hands

Pituitary gland

(pih-TOO-ih-TEHR-ee)

BODY SYSTEM

Sometimes called the "master gland," the pituitary gland secretes hormones that stimulate the other glands of the endocrine system. In this way the pituitary controls such crucial functions as metabolism, growth, and reproduction. A nearby part of the brain, the *hypothalamus* (HIY-poh-THAAL-uh-muhs), signals the pituitary as to which hormones to secrete.

Size and location: A small, oval-shaped gland weighing about one-sixtieth of an ounce, the pituitary is located at the base of the brain. It is normally larger in women than in men and enlarges further during pregnancy.

The pituitary is divided into front (anterior) and rear (posterior) sections, or lobes, that function as entirely different glands.

Role: The pituitary controls most other glands of the endocrine system by secreting a specific hormone to stimulate a particular gland. For example, it can release thyroid-stimulating hormone (TSH) into the bloodstream; TSH tells the thyroid to release more of its hormone thyroxine.

The pituitary's front lobe secretes six or more different hormones that, among other functions, stimulate the thyroid and adrenal glands, control growth (growth hormone), initiate production of breast milk in women (prolactin), and control the development of eggs in the ovaries and sperm in the testes.

The rear lobe releases two hormones. Vasopressin affects the kidneys and thereby controls output of urine. Oxytocin (OK-sih-TOH-sihn) stimulates contractions during childbirth and also controls the release of milk during breast-feeding.

Conditions that affect the pituitary gland: Tumors, serious head injuries, and other factors may cause the pituitary to secrete too little or too much; this affects other endocrine glands and causes various hormonal disorders. The most common problems stem from small tumors that affect particular parts of the gland. Pituitary tumors may also interfere with the optic nerve.

When the pituitary does not secrete enough of one or more hormones, the disorder is called *hypopituitarism* (HIY-poh-pih-TOO-ih-tuh-RIHZ-uhm). In children one form causes hypoglycemia and slows growth, while in adults hypopituitarism can affect the reproductive system and secondary sex characteristics. When the pituitary secretes too little antidiuretic hormone (ADH), diabetes insipidus results. Too little stimulation of the adrenal glands causes a form of Addison's disease.

Secreting too much growth hormone can cause rare disorders such as *acromegaly* (AAK-roh-MEHG-uh-lee). Other hormone disorders, including *Cushing's syndrome,* can also be brought on by overproduction. Too much prolactin leads to impotence and sterility in men and can interrupt menstruation in women.

PKU (phenylketonuria)

(FEHN-uhl-KEET-n-YOOR-ee-uh)

DISEASE

TYPE: GENETIC

See also
Genetic diseases

On the Internet
MARCH OF DIMES
www.marchofdimes.com/
professionals/681_1219.asp

Phenylketonuria (known as PKU for short) is an inherited disease of body chemistry. If it is not recognized early in life, it causes severe developmental disability (mental retardation). Fortunately, however, it can be easily diagnosed and effectively treated, and its adverse effects have become increasingly rare.

Cause: An individual with PKU lacks enough of a specific enzyme (a chemical enabler) to process one of the amino acids found in all proteins. As a result, this amino acid, *phenylalanine* (FEHN-uhl-AAL-uh-NEEN), accumulates in the blood and damages the developing brain.

The inability to produce a sufficient amount of the enzyme is caused by mutations in a single gene. The condition is recessive. That is, the abnormal gene must be inherited from both parents to produce harmful effects in a child.

Incidence: Worldwide, about 350 of every 1 million infants are born with PKU. The disease is relatively common in Caucasians and Asians, and rare in people of African descent.

Noticeable symptoms: If not treated, at three to six months affected babies become less and less responsive to their surroundings. They are irreversibly disabled before one year of age. Affected children are likely to be hyperactive and to have other behavioral problems; some also suffer from seizures. Their skin is likely to be dry and flaky, and their body may have a distinctive musty smell. The pigment-producing cells of skin, eyes, and hair are also altered, so affected children tend to be fair-skinned, blue-eyed, and blond.

Diagnosis: In many countries, the blood of all newborns is routinely tested for excessive phenylalanine. This allows for early identification and early implementation of treatment.

Treatment options: Within the first week to ten days of life an affected baby must go on a diet low in phenylalanine. The diet begins with a special baby formula. The child must then avoid foods such as meat, dairy products, eggs, beans, and nuts that are especially rich in the kinds of protein that contain phenylalanine. Also to be avoided is the common artificial sweetener aspartame, since one of its key ingredients is phenylalanine. In 2000 a panel of experts concluded that the special diet should be maintained for life.

Risk factors: It is especially important for women who have PKU and are of childbearing age to continue a low-phenylalanine diet. A high level of the amino acid in a mother's blood can cause severe developmental disability and other harmful effects in a developing fetus. Furthermore, these effects cannot be reversed by providing the baby with a low-phenylalanine diet after birth.

Placenta
(pluh-SEHN-tuh)

BODY SYSTEM

A developing fetus is nourished by the only temporary organ in the body, the placenta ("flat cake," from its shape).

Size and location: The placenta occupies the uterus along with the fetus and increases in size throughout pregnancy.

Role: The placenta is attached to the wall of the uterus and attached to the fetus by the *umbilical cord*, which brings nutrients and oxygen from the placenta through blood vessels to the fetus and carries wastes from the fetus to the placenta. The capillaries are not connected between the two systems but lie close enough together that oxygen, glucose, and other necessities can flow from the mother's bloodstream into the bloodstream of the placenta. Wastes from the fetus are transferred from the placenta to the mother's blood.

The placenta also has other functions, including production of hormones, especially human chorionic gonadotropin.

When a baby is fully formed, the cervix opens, and the baby passes through the vagina, still attached to its mother by the cord, which is cut at the navel. The placenta also passes through the vagina as *afterbirth* and is discarded.

Conditions that affect the placenta: A physician may note that a tumor is developing from placental tissue because of rapid swelling of the uterus and high blood pressure during pregnancy, although spontaneous abortion may be the first sign of the problem. A blood test of hormones can confirm tumor growth. It is probably a benign tumor called a *hydatidiform mole*. Rarely it may be cancerous. *Consult a physician without delay for irregular vaginal bleeding or excess nausea and vomiting during pregnancy.*

Although benign, a hydatidiform mole can produce dangerous bleeding and must be removed—the embryo is already lost by the time the tumor can be detected. If the growth is removed, no further treatment is needed for a benign tumor except scraping of the uterus in the case of spontaneous abortion, but chemotherapy may be needed for cancer. If the cancer has spread to the walls of the uterus, the uterus may need to be removed. In either case the condition is usually curable.

The placenta may also lie in a position that interferes with birth, necessitating a cesarean section. This is termed *placenta previa*.

Phone doctor

Plague

(PLAYG)

DISEASE

TYPE: INFECTIOUS (BACTERIAL)

In the fourteenth century plague, then known as the Black Death, began to ravage Europe and Asia, killing two out of three inhabitants for the next hundred years, then returning in somewhat smaller epidemics through the eighteenth century. Today plague is much less of a problem. The last plague epidemic in the United States occurred in Los Angeles in 1924.

Cause: A bacterium, *Yersinia pestis*, causes plague. It is commonly found in rodents in certain geographic areas (a "reservoir" of the disease) and passed among them by flea bites. Usually, humans are also infected with plague by fleas from the rodent reservoir, but infection can also occur when animal fluids containing plague bacteria get into an open wound such as a bite from a rodent. When plague has reached the human population, it can be contracted from inhaling droplets expelled by a person with plague in the lungs.

Incidence: Worldwide, about 1,000 to 3,000 cases of plague are reported annually. An average of 13 cases is reported in the United States each year, mainly in the Southwest.

Noticeable symptoms: Three types of plague occur: bubonic (boo-BON-ihk), septicemic (SEHP-tih-SEE-mihk), and pneumonic (noo-MON-ihk). Bubonic plague, an infection of the lymph nodes, is the most common. The lymph nodes become very painful, swollen, and hot to the touch. High fever, severe headache, and exhaustion also occur. If the illness is not treated early, the bacteria can spread to the bloodstream, where they cause blood-clotting problems, fever, shock, and major organ failure; this is septicemic plague. In pneumonic plague, the bacteria spread to the lungs, where they cause coughing, bloody sputum, and breathing difficulties.

Diagnosis: If a person shows the symptoms described above and reports contact with rodents, plague is suspected. A physician will examine the blood and fluid from the lymph nodes. If the person is coughing, a chest x-ray will be ordered. Plague is confirmed by the presence of plague bacteria.

When plague is diagnosed, or even suspected, the physician must report the case to a public health agency. The agency will investigate the case, contact people who might have been exposed, and refer them for treatment. Public health agencies have the authority to put in place the measures to prevent further spread of the disease.

Treatment options: To reduce the risk of death, it is vital that patients receive treatment within 24 hours of the first symptoms. Patients are hospitalized and, particularly if they have pneumonic plague, are isolated from other patients. Treatment consists of antibiotics such as streptomycin or tetracycline. Usually, intravenous fluids and respiratory support are also prescribed.

Prevention: In the United States plague is found in small rodents (usually ground squirrels and rock squirrels) in Colorado and Texas and states to the west. Occasionally, there are outbreaks of active plague. When this happens, national parks and other outdoor recreational areas post notices for visitors to avoid the rodents and check themselves for fleas. Domestic animals can harbor infected fleas when there is an outbreak, and the fleas can then infect nearby humans. A vaccine provides limited protection and should be used before traveling in plague reservoirs. Insect repellents containing DEET applied to clothes or bedding when hiking or camping help prevent flea bites.

Good sanitation is a powerful prevention tool against plague. Eliminating garbage in populated areas reduces the rodent population and, in turn, decreases the likelihood that humans will come in contact with fleas carrying plague. Appropriate use of insecticides to control fleas during a plague outbreak reduces the risk of infection.

Anyone who may have been exposed to plague can be treated with antibiotics as a preventive measure.

Effects on world population and health: With the exception of Australia and Antarctica, where there is no plague, all other continents have plague outbreaks from time to time. A concern in recent years has been the potential of using plague bacteria in germ warfare or a bioterrorist attack; turned into an aerosol, the bacteria could be spread over large populations, causing pneumonic plague—the most deadly form. Researchers are trying to develop vaccines to fight such as possibility

Pleurisy

(PLOOR-ih-see)

SYMPTOM

On the Internet
CENTERS FOR DISEASE CONTROL AND PREVENTION (CDC)
www.cdc.gov/ncidod/dvbid/plague/

Pleurisy produces difficulty in breathing combined with sharp chest pains that worsen when you breathe, signs that tissues covering the lungs are inflamed.

Parts affected: The lungs, diaphragm, and rib cage move as you breathe in and out. These parts are lined with a moist, delicate membrane called the *pleura* (PLOOR-uh). The pleura provides lubrication. This allows the parts to move smoothly across each other and helps make breathing easier. But when the pleura becomes inflamed, chest movement is impeded.

Phone doctor

Related symptoms: Pleurisy is characterized by sharp chest pains that become worse when you cough or breathe deeply. As a result you tend to take rapid, shallow breaths. Other symptoms associated with the underlying disorder may also be present. *See a physician if you suspect pleurisy.* Diagnosis is made from characteristic sounds heard through a stethoscope.

If fluid seeps into the space between the lungs and the rib cage, the condition is called *pleural effusion*. The pain lessens, but breathing becomes even more difficult.

Associations: Pleurisy may be a complication of either injury or disease. Illnesses associated with pleurisy include pneumonia, tuberculosis, rheumatoid arthritis, bronchitis, lupus (systemic lupus erythematosus), and pulmonary embolism. Less commonly, it can result from kidney failure, cancer, viral infections, or the inhalation of asbestos particles (asbestosis).

Relief of symptoms: Pressing against the site of pain can lower pain intensity when coughing. Anti-inflammatory agents and painkillers usually are prescribed, and bed rest is strongly recommended. If the pleurisy is a symptom of bacterial infection, it is effectively treated with antibiotics. If fluid is present in the space around the lungs, it will be removed by inserting a thin needle between the ribs.

Plumbism

See **Lead poisoning**

PMS (premenstrual syndrome)

(pree-MEHN-stroo-uhl)

DISEASE

TYPE: HORMONAL

Premenstrual syndrome (PMS) consists of the physical and psychological sensations experienced by some women for several days before a menstrual period. The woman may feel tense, exhausted, bloated, and moody and experience headaches and backaches. Symptoms disappear when the menstrual flow begins.

Cause: The amounts of estrogen and progesterone hormones carried throughout a woman's body by the circulatory system vary during the course of a menstrual cycle. These fluctuations can result in the various physical and emotional changes of PMS. For example, estrogen causes tissues to retain fluids, leading to bloating, breast tenderness, and weight gain.

Practice meditation

No caffeine

Exercise

12-Step meeting

Incidence: As many as one-third of all menstruating women experience premenstrual syndrome to some extent. Usually, the symptoms are mild and last only a brief time. In about one out of ten cases, however, the symptoms are severe, long-lasting, and disabling.

Noticeable symptoms: Common behavioral symptoms of PMS include nervousness, mood swings, insomnia, lethargy, and irritability. Physical symptoms include abdominal bloating, breast tenderness or swelling, headaches, backaches, appetite changes, and weight gain. These usually begin five to ten days before menstruation and disappear within a few hours after the onset of menstruation.

Women who have respiratory problems, such as asthma, may find that these problems become worse during the premenstrual period. Acne, epilepsy, and varicose veins also may be aggravated.

Diagnosis: A physician will probably ask if there have been any other difficulties related to menstruation. Blood tests may be conducted to check estrogen and progesterone levels.

Treatment options: Treatment of PMS is generally limited to relieving symptoms. Tranquilizers, antidepressants, sedatives, diuretics, or vitamins may be prescribed. Stress reduction techniques and regular exercise may be recommended. Dietary changes, including avoiding stimulants such as caffeine, help some women. If the doctor suspects that emotional problems are contributing to PMS, the patient may be advised to obtain psychological counseling. The doctor may also suggest joining a self-help group for women with PMS.

Pneumoconiosis   *See* **Environment and disease**

Pneumocystis carinii pneumonia
(NOO-muh-SIHS-tihs kuh-RIY-nee-iy)

DISEASE

TYPE: INFECTIOUS (PARASITIC)

People who are infected with HIV (the virus that causes AIDS), who have had organ transplants, or who are on chemotherapy are especially vulnerable to *Pneumocystis*.

See also
HIV and AIDS
Immune system
Opportunistic diseases
Parasites and disease
Pneumonia

On the Internet
AMERICAN ACADEMY
OF FAMILY PHYSICIANS
familydoctor.org/475.xml

Cause: *Pneumocystis carinii* is an unusual microscopic fungus that causes *Pneumocystis carinii* pneumonia (PCP). *Pneumocystis* is found in the respiratory tracts of most humans and many animals. It coexists peacefully with humans with normal immune systems but grows out of control, causing pneumonia, in individuals with immune system problems.

Incidence: Before the onset of the AIDS epidemic in 1981, PCP was very rare. It has since become a common cause of illness and death in people whose immune system is compromised, especially those with AIDS. In the United States, it affects about 60% of AIDS patients during the course of their illness; it is three times more common in white patients than black patients.

Noticeable symptoms: PCP usually appears with a low-grade fever, dry cough, weight loss, and fatigue. More severe symptoms—including respiratory failure and cyanosis (bluish skin and lips from lack of oxygen)—may also occur, particularly if the infection is not treated promptly.

Diagnosis: Pneumonia of any type is diagnosed by listening to the lungs with a stethoscope, then taking an x-ray of the lungs. If a person is at risk for PCP, a doctor may assume that *Pneumocystis* is the cause of the illness and begin appropriate treatment. Identifying *Pneumocystis* requires a biopsy—removal and examination of tissue from the respiratory tract or lungs.

Treatment options: Hospitalization is required during treatment for all but mild cases. Antimicrobial medication, preferably trimethoprim-sulfamethoxazole, is given orally or intravenously. Corticosteroids are often used as well.

Prophylactic therapy—giving medication to prevent illness—reduces the risk of developing PCP.

Pneumonia
(noo-MOHN-yuh)

DISEASE

TYPE: INFECTIOUS (BACTERIAL);
    CHEMICAL

Pneumonia is inflammation of tissues in the lungs. Over 50 specific diseases can result in pulmonary inflammation, or pneumonia. One serious form is viral pneumonia, which is treated in a separate entry. Other common causes are various fungal diseases, including *Pneumocystis carinii* pneumonia. The present entry is concerned with bacterial pneumonia and noninfectious pneumonia.

On the Internet
KIDS HEALTH
kidshealth.org/parent/infections/
lung/pneumonia.html

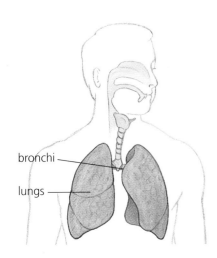

Any disease that produces inflammation of one or both lungs is known as pneumonia. Most pneumonias caused by bacteria are easily cured with antibiotics when they are diagnosed and treated.

Parts affected: One of the milder pneumonias is called *bronchial pneumonia*. The area inflamed with this disease is relatively small and tends to center around the major air passageways of the lungs (bronchi). When very mild, this form is sometimes nicknamed "walking pneumonia," since the patient does not feel sufficiently ill to seek medical help or even to go to bed until after several weeks of symptoms.

Pneumonias often affect a larger area than the bronchial tubes, however, and when an entire lobe of a lung becomes inflamed, the patient is said to have *lobar pneumonia*. If parts of both lungs have become inflamed, the patient is said to have *double pneumonia*.

Cause: Pneumococcal pneumonia caused by the bacterium *Streptococcus pneumoniae* (also known as *Pneumococcus, Diplococcus pneumoniae*, and various other names—the bacterium was not firmly identified until the 1970s) accounts for about 90% of all pneumonias resulting from bacterial infection. Among other bacterial pneumonias are Legionnaires' disease and mycoplasmal pneumonia, a relatively mild pneumonia caused by *Mycoplasma pneumoniae* that chiefly afflicts young adults in the summer and fall. Several bacteria that may also invade the lungs and cause pneumonia include, among others, *Hemophilus influenzae, Staphylococcus aureus*, and *Escherichia coli*.

Hospital-acquired (nosocomial) pneumonia is pneumonia acquired after a patient has entered the hospital. The distinction is made because people who have been hospitalized with serious diseases sometimes die of pneumonia contracted at the hospital. Nosocomial pneumonia is the second leading cause of infection in patients admitted for other disorders.

In addition to the infectious pneumonias there are various lung inflammations with different origins. *Aspiration pneumonia* can be caused by inhaling foods, liquids, chemical irritants, or other substances into the lungs. This can happen when an unconscious person vomits and inadvertently inhales some partly digested food. Other noninfectious pneumonias may be caused by an allergy or an autoimmune disease, such as rheumatoid arthritis. This form, called *interstitial* (IHN-tuhr-STIHSH-uhl) *pneumonia*, may also be accompanied by other signs, such as clubbing of the ends of the fingers and shrinkage of the lungs.

Incidence: In the United States, about 1.2 million people are hospitalized each year with community-acquired pneumonia; bacteria, especially *Streptococcus pneumoniae*, are the most common cause. The majority of cases respond well to treatment. Nonetheless, together with influenza, pneumonia is the leading cause of infectious death in the country.

People most at risk of contracting pneumonia are hospitalized patients, adults over age 65, very young children, and those of any age with serious illnesses or weakened immune systems.

Noticeable symptoms: In most cases the first symptoms of pneumonia are fever, chills, and cough, often combined with shortness of breath, even while resting. Mild pneumonias in healthy people, such as mycoplasmal pneumonia, may have essentially the same symptoms as a cold and can be "walking pneumonias." But lobar and other pneumonias that are more serious tend to strike more suddenly and to produce more severe symptoms—including chest pain, blood in the sputum, a high fever, and delirium. The patient's pulse and respiration rates can rise to nearly twice normal. *If you suspect even a mild case of pneumonia, consult your physician as soon as possible.*

Diagnosis: The breathing of a person with pneumonia creates sounds that, when a doctor listens through a stethoscope, indicate that an inflammation of lung tissue is present. A chest x-ray and tests of sputum and of a blood sample may be necessary to diagnose the type and severity of pneumonia. In some cases the physician may also look for areas of inflammation directly by means of a *bronchoscope*. This instrument is a fiber-optic tube that is passed through the mouth or nose into the lungs. It allows the doctor to view the inside of the respiratory tract to pinpoint areas of inflammation.

Treatment options: For most bacterial pneumonias antibiotics are the preferred remedy, often penicillin or erythromycin, administered for a week or two. If the pneumonia is fairly extensive and the patient is having trouble breathing, oxygen will probably be administered with an oxygen mask. Hospitalization may be required.

Prevention: A vaccine against pneumococcal pneumonia can provide protection for three to five years in many patients. The vaccine is especially recommended for those most susceptible

Phone doctor

to pneumonia, including people over 65, people with heart or lung problems, with an immune-deficiency disease, or problems with alcoholism.

Pneumothorax　　*See* **Lungs**

Poisoning

Poisons are substances that can disrupt normal functioning of the body, causing life-threatening medical problems. Poisoning often depends on the amount of the substance taken in and the individual. For example, iron-containing supplements are a leading cause of poisoning deaths for children under age six.

Cause: Poisons generally disrupt bodily functions in one of four different ways. *Irritants,* such as copper sulfate, arsenic, and salts of lead, inflame mucous membranes. *Blood toxins,* such as carbon monoxide, act on the blood cells to deprive the body of life-giving oxygen. *Nerve toxins*—including cocaine and other narcotics, barbiturates, nicotine patches or gum, and even alcohol—poison the system by affecting nerves or certain cell processes. Many organic poisons, such as snake venom or fungal poisons, are in this class. *Corrosive poisons,* such as ammonia, lye, and sulfuric acid, attack and destroy bodily tissues directly.

Many poisons are double-acting. Lead salts and some fungal poisons not only irritate tissues but also act as nerve toxins. All corrosive poisons are irritants in smaller amounts.

Incidence: Children under age six are most at risk, mainly because they are so curious and so prone to putting almost anything they find into their mouths. Each year in the United States, more than 1 million young children are accidentally poisoned; 90% of those poisonings happen in the home. Counting people of all ages, the nation has about 14,000 deaths from accidental poisoning and 5,000 from suicide poisoning each year.

Noticeable symptoms: Different poisons produce widely different symptoms. If you are uncertain if someone has swallowed a poison, the following may help you find out.

■ Sudden illness and a nearby bottle of a poisonous substance or medication.

■ Stains or odors on the clothing or near where the victim

was playing or working. The smell of gasoline, lighter fluid, or other chemicals on the breath is another telling sign of swallowed poison.

- Burns or redness on the lips and around the mouth.
- Pain or burning in the mouth or throat.
- Signs of eating leaves or berries.
- Nausea or vomiting.
- Vision problems, confused state, convulsions, or unconsciousness.

Call an emergency hot line if you suspect a poisoning has occurred. In the United States, the national number is

1-800-222-1222.

List the number with other emergency numbers near your telephone or inside the front cover of your telephone book. If outside the United States, learn the local hot line number.

Poison gases pose special problems since nothing obvious has been ingested. Unexplained sleepiness or headache can be an early sign of carbon monoxide poisoning. Although household natural gas contains an unpleasant scent, some people gradually become used to it and fail to recognize a steady buildup of gas. If you enter a room and find one or more persons who have passed out, suspect a poison gas, and call for help. Take care not to become overcome by the gas yourself.

Diagnosis: The poison-control center will ask a series of questions concerning the incident and type of poison involved. If possible, have the container that held the poison handy because the center may want you to read information from the label. The center will then tell you what steps to take.

Treatment options: Prompt first aid for poisoning cases is very important, but do not take steps before calling the poison-control center. If at all possible, identify the cause of the poisoning before you call. Follow directions for treatment. Call an ambulance, or take the patient to the hospital as soon as possible.

First aid: If you cannot reach a poison control hot line or a hospital emergency service, you may *with caution* employ certain first aid steps on your own. For swallowed poisons start by giving the victim water or milk to drink—unless the patient is unconscious, semiconscious, or experiencing seizures.

Poison control

Read label

Call ambulance

If you are unsure what poison was taken, do not induce vomiting. At one time, it was recommended that vomiting be induced with syrup of ipecac, an over-the-counter drug found in many first aid kits. This is no longer recommended. Studies have shown that the medication can actually make certain poisoning situations worse. Additionally, inducing vomiting, particularly in children, increases their risk of accidentally inhaling vomited material into the lungs. Anyone having syrup of ipecac in the home is advised to dispose of it by flushing it down the toilet.

If the poison has a specific antidote and you have it, administer it. Otherwise, activated charcoal can be given to help absorb the toxin even if you are unsure which poison was swallowed; however, it is not effective for insecticide or alcohol poisoning.

For inhaled poisons, such as carbon monoxide, get the patient into fresh air as soon as possible. Be careful that you are not overcome by the gases as well. If the person is not breathing, and you are trained to do so, administer cardiopulmonary resuscitation (CPR). Keep the patient warm by wrapping him or her in blankets until medical assistance arrives.

Use CPR

Lock any potentially dangerous household chemicals or medicines where children cannot get them. Store all medicines separately from any foods and high above the reach of any young children who might visit.

For external contamination of the skin by poisons, wash the affected area repeatedly with fresh water. Take off any clothing contaminated by the chemical.

Prevention: You can take a number of steps to prevent accidental poisonings, especially in households with small children. Store all medicines, household cleaners, garden chemicals, and other poisonous substances on a high shelf or, better yet, in a locked cabinet. Never store poisonous substances alongside food items. Keep poisons in their original containers and do not reuse the containers. Always close containers of medicines and poisons as soon as you finish using them. Be aware that "child-resistant" packaging does not mean "child-proof."

Teach children about the dangers of poisons. Don't equate medicine with candy. Follow medicine label directions careful-

Don't eat the . . .

Many common garden plants and shrubs, and even some wild flowers, are poisonous. As a general rule it is best not to eat leaves and berries of any plants unless you are absolutely certain they are harmless. Some common plants and plant parts that are poisonous are listed below.

Plant	Poisonous Part
apple	seeds
buttercup	all
cherry	pits
coleus	all
daffodil	bulbs
English ivy	all
holly	berries
lily of the valley	all
mistletoe	berries
mushroom, wild	various species; avoid unless you are certain they are safe
peach	pits
poinsettia	all
potato	roots, vines, sprouts, and green parts on tubers
rhododendron	all
tomato	leaves
yew	needles and berries

ly to avoid accidental overdoses. Never leave alcoholic drinks untended. Keep on hand activated charcoal for absorbing poisons that have no specific antidote.

Every home should have smoke and carbon monoxide detectors mounted on the ceiling in or near bedrooms. Oil or gas furnaces should receive regular servicing.

Poison ivy, oak, sumac

Phone doctor

Poison ivy, poison oak, and poison sumac are three common North American plants that contain the same oily resin that gives most people an itchy, red rash whenever it touches their skin. The rash, a form of *contact dermatitis,* usually only causes minor discomfort and clears up completely. But *in cases of extensive or unusual exposure—such as in the eyes or lungs—see your doctor.*

Size and location: People living in or visiting North America need to learn to recognize and avoid these plants.

Poison ivy: This plant is common in the northern United States. It grows as a low, woody weed along fences, stone walls, paths, and roads or as a long hairy vine growing up a tree. Its most distinctive feature—shared with poison oak—is that it has three glossy leaves, one at the end of the stem and two opposite each other just below it.

Poison oak: One form is most often found in southern states and a taller species on the West Coast as far north as Canada. It is related to poison ivy and not to the oak tree, but its three leaves look a lot like glossy versions of those of an oak tree.

Poison sumac: This is a small tree found in swampy areas in the eastern United States. Because of its habitat, it is comparatively rare. It normally grows to about five or six feet tall. Nonpoisonous sumacs have red berries, while poison sumac has green or white berries.

Cause: All three of these plants cause contact dermatitis because they contain an oil resin called *urushiol* (oo-ROO-shee-OHL). The resin can be found on all parts of the plant, including the leaves, stem, roots, and even the berries. For most people even accidentally brushing against the leaves of one of these plants transfers enough urushiol to their skin to

See also
Allergies
Rashes

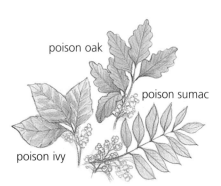

poison oak

poison sumac

poison ivy

The most important way to prevent the itchy rash of common poison plants is to learn to recognize the plants and avoid them. If you are exposed, do not scratch the itch but use soothing medications. Long sleeves and trousers can help prevent exposure (although they can carry the poison until they are washed) or they can help keep you from scratching rashes on your arms and legs.

Emergency Room

cause a severe allergic reaction. Since the offending substance is the same in all three plants, if you are sensitive to poison ivy, you will also be sensitive to poison oak and poison sumac.

Incidence: Though estimates vary, as many as four out of five Americans are sensitive to urushiol. Reaction to urushiol is among the most common causes of contact dermatitis, which may affect as many as 50 million Americans each year.

Noticeable symptoms: After contact with one of these plants your skin will redden visibly in the affected area and become quite itchy. Later small bumps and blisters will form.

Treatment options: Calamine lotion, over-the-counter hydrocortisone cream, or another preparation specifically formulated for poison ivy may be applied to the affected area. A doctor can prescribe a prescription-strength hydrocortisone medication along with an antihistamine.

Open blisters should be protected from possible infection. A loose covering may help keep a person from scratching, but do not bandage tightly.

Prevention: Staying away from poison plants is the best way to prevent the rash. A helpful rhyme is

If leaves are three,
Then let it be.

Keeping the skin covered with clothing can prevent contact in the first place. Over-the-counter lotions and creams that form a protective barrier against accidental contact are available.

A person can lessen or eliminate altogether the effects of accidental contact by washing affected skin thoroughly within five to ten minutes after contact.

Remember that a person can also get a rash by touching clothing or yard tools that have urushiol on them and that the urushiol can remain active for up to a year. Contaminated clothing should be washed thoroughly. ***Never burn any part of these three plants.*** Smoke can transport urushiol, causing serious internal and external problems for those who are in its path. Inhaling such smoke is especially dangerous; if you think you have inhaled smoke from burning one of these plants, contact a doctor immediately.

Poliomyelitis ("polio")

(POH-lee-oh-MIY-uh-LIY-tihs)

> **Did You Know?**
> The first polio vaccine was developed in the early 1950s by microbiologist Jonas Salk. The first volunteers to receive the vaccine included Salk, his wife, and their three children.

Poliomyelitis, familiarly known as polio, is an infectious disease that affects the central nervous system. In its more serious form, it causes paralysis—the inability to move muscles. There is no cure, but vaccines effectively prevent the disease. A global campaign of vaccination, launched in 1988, has made great strides toward its goal of eradicating poliomyelitis.

Cause: Polio is caused by any one of three different polioviruses. The viruses, which are highly contagious, are spread by person-to-person contact, contact with infected secretions from the nose or mouth, or contact with infected feces (usually as a result of poor hand washing or ingestion of contaminated food or water). Once in the body, the viruses multiply in the intestine and invade the nervous system.

Incidence: Once called infantile paralysis, polio primarily affects children, particularly those under age five. However, the risk for paralysis from the virus increases with age. Risk of paralysis is also higher among people who are under stress.

Worldwide, because of the global effort to eradicate the disease, polio cases have decreased over 99% since 1988, from more than 350,000 cases to fewer than 2,000 annually.

In the United States, no known infectious cases occurred between 1979 and 2005—a significant advance since 1952, when the nation had nearly 58,000 known cases, with more than one-third of the individuals developing paralysis. But in 2005, five cases occurred among unvaccinated children in a small Minnesota community. Over the years, a low number of non-infectious cases have resulted from an oral vaccine that is no longer recommended for use.

Noticeable symptoms: In its mildest form the disease symptoms are fever, headache, nausea, and vomiting, which last for only a few hours. In its longer-lasting form symptoms also include irritation of the membranes that line the brain as well as stiffness in the neck and back.

The form of polio that causes paralysis begins with the same mild symptoms, which then go away. However, several days later the symptoms return, and the patient feels muscle pain and weakness as paralysis begins.

Treatment options: There is no cure for poliomyelitis. Treatment involves rest, liquids, and time. If paralysis occurs, hospitalization is required and steps may need to be taken to keep the patient breathing. After the active stage of the disease is over, the patient needs to rebuild strength and muscle tone through physical therapy to avoid more permanent damage. Depending on the extent to which muscles have been affected by the disease, the patient may regain muscle tone and movement completely or retain some degree of paralysis. In some cases, symptoms return years later, long after it appears that the disease has been completely eliminated from the body.

Polycystic kidney disease

(POL-ee-SIHS-tihk)

DISEASE

TYPE: GENETIC

See also
Aneurysm
Bladder infections
Cysts
Diverticular diseases
Genetic diseases
Hypertension
Kidney diseases
Kidneys
Liver
Prolapse of mitral valve

On the Internet
NATIONAL KIDNEY AND UROLOGIC DISEASES INFORMATION CLEARINGHOUSE
kidney.niddk.nih.gov/kudiseases/pubs/polycystic

Polycystic kidney disease refers to disorders that arise when the kidneys develop fluid-filled sacs, or cysts. The two most common varieties are "autosomal," meaning that they are genetic diseases whose cause is a gene that is not on one of the sex-determining chromosomes. Symptoms of the more common of the two, *autosomal dominant polycystic kidney disease* (ADPKD), seldom become apparent before the third or fourth decade of life. Symptoms of the much less common *autosomal recessive polycystic disease* (ARPKD) appear much earlier, in babies and children.

The form that affects usually children, ARPKD, is by far the more serious of the two. Before birth the disease may adversely affect development of the lungs, so that 30 to 50% of newborns with the disease die of severe breathing difficulties. The kidneys fail in about one in three affected children by the age of ten.

The form that affects adults, by contrast, varies enormously in its impact. Many have no noticeable symptoms.

Cause: As the name indicates, autosomal dominant polycystic kidney disease is caused by a single, dominant gene, most often a gene on chromosome 16.

Autosomal recessive PKD is caused by a pair of recessive genes on chromosome 6.

In both forms of the disease a large number of fluid-filled sacs called cysts develop in the kidneys, making them abnormally large and gradually hindering their function. Both forms tend to be progressive, and many of those affected eventually suffer kidney failure.

Both forms often affect other body organs and systems as well. Among the more common complications are cysts in the liver, high blood pressure, malfunction (prolapse) of the mitral valve in the heart, frequent kidney and bladder infections, aneurysms (bulges) in the blood vessels of the brain, and pockets (diverticula) in the walls of the large intestine.

Incidence: ADPKD is very common, affecting between 1 in 400 to 1 in 500 people. It is a leading form of kidney disease, and about 600,000 people in the United States and 12.5 million worldwide are believed to have it at any given time, making it the most common known genetic disease.

ARPKD—the childhood form—is much rarer, affecting about 1 in 10,000 births.

Noticeable symptoms: Common symptoms of polycystic kidney disease include pain in the back and sides, blood in the urine, excessive urination at night, persistent headache, and susceptibility to kidney and bladder infections.

Diagnosis: An early sign of the disease, which may appear on routine medical examination, is hypertension (high blood pressure), triggered by hormones released by the damaged kidneys. The cysts are usually apparent on ultrasound images.

No caffeine   Avoid aspirin

Treatment options: Neither form of the disease can be cured, except by kidney transplant. But treatment can alleviate its symptoms, possibly slow its progress, and control some of its complications. Affected individuals are advised to avoid caffeine and nonsteroidal anti-inflammatory painkillers such as aspirin.

High blood pressure is controlled with diet and medications. Infections are treated with antibiotics, although only certain of these drugs can penetrate cysts. Surgery can sometimes reduce cysts, but the relief is only temporary.

Outlook: Both forms of the disease tend to be progressive. Most of those with ARPKD and about half of those with ADPKD will eventually suffer complete kidney failure, requiring either regular dialysis or a kidney transplant. On the other hand, ADPKD is often so mild that the symptoms are overlooked or easily controlled.

Polycythemia

(POL-ee-siy-THEE-mee-uh)

DISEASE

TYPE: UNKNOWN

See also
Blood
Embolism
Heart attack
Leukemia
Nosebleed
Stem cells
Stroke
Thrombophlebitis

On the Internet
THE LEUKEMIA AND LYMPHOMA
SOCIETY
www.leukemia-lymphoma.org/
all_mat_toc.adp?item_id=9955

In some people for reasons that are poorly understood, some stem cells in their bone marrow begin to produce far too many blood cells, a disease called polycythemia ("many blood cells"). This disease is recognized by a very large number of red blood cells observed in blood samples. Numbers of white blood cells and platelets increase abnormally as well. The disease is also known as primary polycythemia, polycythemia vera ("true"), or polycythemia ruba ("red") vera.

A condition known as secondary polycythemia occurs when heart disease, pulmonary disease, cancer, smoking, and exposure to high altitudes for a long period of time (mountain sickness) reduce oxygen concentration in the blood, leading the bone marrow to produce extra red blood cells.

Incidence: Primary polycythemia is a rare disease, with about 1 person in a million likely to develop it. Although it can occur at any age, it usually develops between the ages of 50 and 70.

Noticeable symptoms: Because the excess blood cells slow blood flow and reduce delivery of oxygen, headaches, dizziness, fatigue, weakness, and visual disturbances are common. Slow blood flow can also result in high blood pressure, leg cramps, or heart pain. The excess in platelets can produce both bleeding and blood clots. Severe itching after bathing in hot water is common.

Diagnosis: An elevated red blood cell count coupled with an enlarged spleen (an organ that destroys worn-out red blood cells) are major signs of polycythemia.

Treatment options: Polycythemia is usually treated with a procedure called phlebotomy (flih-BOT-uh-mee), in which an incision is made in a vein and a pint or so of blood is removed. This procedure is repeated—usually once a week—until the red blood cell count is reduced to a normal range. The treatment thins the blood and removes excess red cells. Chemotherapy is sometimes used to prevent leukemia from developing.

Stages and progress: Polycythemia progresses slowly and patients receiving proper treatment usually do well. Left untreated, primary polycythemia increases the risk of embolism and can sometimes induce a form of leukemia.

INDEX

The first digit in **boldface** is the volume number; page numbers follow the colon.
Page numbers in **boldface** indicate entries.

A

Abdominal wall defects **2**:98
Abrasions **8**:115
Abruptio placentae **7**:5, **7**:9, **7**:13
Abscess **1**:9–10, **2**:16–17, **7**:36
Acetaminophen **6**:58
Achalasia **2**:56, **3**:102
Achilles tendon **8**:66
Achondroplasia **4**:53, **4**:104
Acid reflux **4**:40
Acne **1**:10–12
Acoustic neuroma **3**:52, **8**:83
Acromegaly **4**:104, **6**:99
ACTH (adrenocorticotropic
    hormone) **4**:102
Actinomycetes **1**:97
Acupuncture **1**:35, **1**:36, **6**:59
Acute inflammatory
    polyneuropathy. *See*
    Guillain-Barré syndrome
Acute lymphocytic leukemia
    5:55
Acute nonlymphocytic
    leukemia **5**:55
Acute porphyrias **7**:2–4
Acute pyelonephritis **5**:34
Acyclovir **2**:88, **4**:36
ADA deficiency **1**:12–13
Addiction **3**:57, **3**:59–60
Addison's disease **1**:17, **1**:90,
    4:104, **4**:106, **8**:20
Adenine **4**:37
Adenoids **6**:27, **8**:62
Adenoma **8**:83
Adenomyosis **3**:90
Adenosine deaminase. *See* ADA
    deficiency
Adenoviruses **1**:87, **8**:102
ADH (antidiuretic hormone)
    3:29, **4**:103, **6**:99
ADHD (attention-deficit/
    hyperactivity disorder)
    1:13–15, **5**:48
Adolescence **4**:54, **4**:56
Adrenal glands **1**:16–17, **3**:89
Adrenaline. *See* Epinephrine
Adult acne. *See* Rosacea
Adulthood **1**:17–18, **4**:53
Adult stem cells **8**:17
Aedes aegypti (mosquito) **3**:20
Aerobic exercise, **3**:105
African sleeping sickness **6**:72
Afterbirth. *See* Placenta
Agent Orange **2**:65

Aging **1**:17–20
    shingles, **7**:80
Agoraphobia **6**:63
Agranulocytes **6**:92
Agranulocytosis **6**:25
AIDS (acquired
    immunodeficiency
    syndrome). *See* HIV and
    AIDS
AIDS dementia **4**:98
Air sac **5**:65
Albinism **1**:21–22, **7**:103
Alcohol
    and cancer **2**:35
    fetal alcohol syndrome **1**:26,
    3:116–17
    and frostbite **4**:19–20
    nausea from **6**:15
Alcoholics Anonymous **1**:23,
    1:25, **5**:100
Alcoholism **1**:22–27
    alcoholic siderosis **7**:86
    and cirrhosis of the liver
    2:75
    delirium tremens **1**:23,
    3:16–17
    dementia **3**:19–20
    Korsakoff's syndrome **1**:42
    pancreatitis **6**:62–63
    paranoia **6**:68
Alcohol poisoning **1**:22
ALD (adrenoleukodystrophy)
    1:27–28
Aldosterone **1**:16, **4**:102
Allele **4**:38
Allergens **1**:28–32, **1**:74, **4**:61
Allergic contact dermatitis **7**:34
Allergic purpura **7**:27
Allergic rhinitis. *See* Hay fever
Allergies **1**:28–32
    from animals **6**:89
    asthma **1**:73–77
    hay fever **1**:29, **4**:61–63
    and immune system **5**:3
    and itching **5**:24
    to stings **8**:18–19
Allodynia **7**:80
Allograft **6**:41
Alper, Tikva **7**:15
ALS (amyotrophic lateral
    sclerosis) **1**:32–35, **6**:65
Alternative medicine **1**:35–37
Altitude sickness. *See*
    Polycythemia
Alveoli **2**:109, **3**:82–83, **5**:65, **7**:39

Alzheimer, Alois **1**:39
Alzheimer's disease **1**:37–40
    dementia **3**:19–20
Amblyopia **3**:108
Amebic dysentery **1**:9, **3**:60–62,
    6:72
Amenorrhea **1**:40–41
Amino acids **4**:38
Amnesia **1**:41–43, **2**:96
Amniocentesis **2**:70, **3**:36
Amniotic fluid **3**:117–18,
    7:11–12
Amphetamines **3**:58
Amyloidosis **8**:31–32
Amyotrophic lateral sclerosis.
    See ALS
Anabolism, **5**:102
Analgesia **7**:78
Analgesics, **5**:89
Anal itching **5**:24
Anaphylactic shock **1**:30, **7**:83,
    8:31
Anaphylaxis **5**:42
Anemia(s) **1**:43–47, **3**:115
    aplastic **1**:44–45
    pernicious **1**:44, **8**:20
    in pregnancy **7**:8
    thalassemia **1**:44, **8**:46–47
    See also Sickle cell anemia
Anencephaly **6**:22
Anesthetics, local **6**:59
Aneurysm **1**:47–49, **2**:75, **5**:23,
    8:26
Angina **1**:50–51, **2**:40
Angiogram **1**:79
Angiography **3**:75–76
Angioplasty **1**:80, **4**:77
Animal bites **1**:54, **6**:91
    snakebites **7**:112–14
    spider bites **8**:1–2
Animal diseases and humans
    1:51–55
    anthrax **1**:54, **1**:58–61
    cryptosporidiosis **3**:4–5
    Q fever **7**:29
    rabies **1**:51, **1**:53, **6**:89,
    7:30–31
    SARS **7**:62–63
    tularemia **8**:82
    See also Pets and disease
Animal models **1**:54
Ankylosing spondylitis **1**:93,
    1:95
Anopheles mosquito **5**:79
Anorexia nervosa **1**:55–58

Anosmia **6**:27, **7**:78
Ant **8**:19
Antacids **5**:89
Antegrade amnesia **1**:41
Anterior compartment
    syndrome **4**:17
Anthracosis **3**:94
Anthrax **1**:54, **1**:58–61
    bioterrorism **3**:81
Antibiotics **5**:90
    for gonorrhea **4**:49–50
    for infants **5**:9
Antibodies **5**:2–3, **5**:74, **6**:92–93
    in rheumatoid arthritis **7**:46
Anticoagulants **3**:76
Anticonvulsants **3**:100, **6**:58
Antidepressants **5**:90, **6**:58
Antidiuretic hormone. *See* ADH
Antigens **1**:30, **6**:41
Antihistamines **4**:62, **4**:99, **5**:90
Antihypertensives **5**:90
Anti-inflammatory drugs **6**:58
Antipsychotic drugs **7**:68–69
Antiretrovirals **4**:97
Antivenin **7**:113
Anus **2**:98, **3**:47, **7**:35
Anuscope **4**:84
Anxiety **1**:61–63, **5**:99
Aorta **1**:69, **6**:78–79
    coarctation of **2**:103
    overriding of **2**:103
    transposition of great vessels
    2:103–4
Aortic aneurysm **1**:47–49
Aortic stenosis **2**:102–3, **4**:68
Aortic valve **2**:102–3
Aphasia **1**:63–64
Aphthous ulcer **2**:38
Aplastic anemia **1**:44–45
Aplastic crisis **7**:85
Apnea **2**:61
    See also Sleep apnea
Apocrine glands **3**:107
Apoplexy. *See* Stroke
Appendicitis **1**:64–66, **3**:48,
    8:21
Appendicular skeleton **7**:95
Appendix **5**:40
Appert, Nicolas-Francis **4**:10
Aqueous humor **4**:45
Arachnids **6**:70
Arboviruses **8**:79–80, **8**:102
Arenaviruses **8**:102
Aristotle **2**:15
Aromatherapy **1**:36

Our thanks to the following organizations and persons who made the photographs used in this set possible:

Christ Episcopal Church Youth Program (Mary Millan)
Maryknoll Lay Missioners (Jean Walsh)
Mount Vernon Teen Task Force (Chris Webb)
Putnam Family Support and Advocacy, Inc. (Pam Forde)

Photography assistant: Tania Gandy-Collins

MODELS
Roland Benson, Diana Brenner, Sally Bunch, Deirdre Burke, Kevin Chapin, Michael Clarke, Michelle Collins, Bryan Duggan, Germaine Elvy, Eugene Ehrlich, Caitlin Faughnan, Irmgard Kallenbach, Max Lipson, Lydia McCarthy, Amanda Moradel, Joshua Moradel, Veronica Moradel, Kate Peckham, Sara Pettinger, Micaela Rich, Mario Salinas, Heather Scogna, Halima Simmons, Wendy Sinclair, Barbara Totten, T.J. Trancynger, Rolando Walker, Jean Walsh, Hannah Walsh-Regotti, Maria Walsh-Regotti, Deborah Whelan, Gregory Whelan, Francis Wick, Elaine Young, Leanne Young